care about prayer, and I know you do, this book is one of the best I've read.

—Terry Law
Author, founder, and president of
World Compassion Ministries

Cameron's latest book about prayer, *40 Days Through the Prayers of Jesus*, is on time. In our busy world we must be reminded that Christ established prayer as our one-on-one link to Him. Unlike the technology we have come to love, with prayer there are no buttons to push, nothing to tap, no dead zones, and no batteries to charge. Prayer, as always, demands our time and emotional presence. Thank you, Tim, for reminding me of the world of prayer I encountered while growing up. Thanks for bringing me back.

—Clifton L. Taulbert
International speaker
Best-selling author of *Eight Habits of the Heart*

ve known Tim Cameron and of him most of my life
gh various academic, family, and professional con-
ns. If you want to know someone, don't just listen to
hey say, but watch what they do. Tim Cameron has
served as a role model to me and many others in this
milarly, if we want to know how to pray and commu-
ith God, we need only follow the examples we have
en. In this book, *40 Days Through the Prayers of*
lays out the road map provided for us all.

—Jim Stovall
Best-selling author of *The Ultimate Gift*

1) "La foi, ce n'
c'est l'erga
la persévér
l'oeuvre!

2) The Lord is able to speak loudly enough to get through to me!

3) There is NO disease above the Lord.

4) Luke 18:27

Tim Cameron takes us to the source of all true prayer—the words and example of Jesus Christ Himself. It's a refreshingly simple approach. What better teacher could there be? And what greater arena for growth? The prayers of Jesus powerfully shape our world to this day, and here is your invitation to join in.

—Pete Greig

Cofounder of 24-7 Prayer Internationa

Author of Red Moon Rising and Dirty Glo

40 Days Through the Prayers of Jesus is a compelling i
tion into a deeper intimacy with God. As Tim Ca
shows you how vital prayer was to Jesus, you'll fi
self hungering for a greater connection yourself.
longer see prayer as a rigid obligation but as an
lifestyle of engagement with Jesus and the Fath
everything else about life into perspective. T
you won't want to miss!

—V

Author

and coauti

From Jesus's first recorded prayer at Hi
the Jordan as the heavens opened an
on Jesus, to the dramatic prayer on
God, why have You forsaken Me?,"
us an incisive look into the pray
book, 40 Days Through the Pr
enjoyed day 36, "Forgiving Ev
don't give forgiveness, you do

I ha
thro
necti
what
always
way. Si
nicate w
been giv
Jesus, Tir

Tim Cameron does an amazing job uncovering Jesus's examples of prayer in His Word and using them to lead and encourage us in our own daily prayer lives. His book, *40 Days Through the Prayers of Jesus*, teaches why, when, where, and how we have been called to pray based on God's Scripture. I trust that if you are looking for a deeper relationship with your heavenly Father, this will be a great instrument to assist you on that journey!

—Joe White
President of Kanakuk Ministries

I have known Tim since college. I thoroughly enjoyed reading from this book, *40 Days Through the Prayers of Jesus*. He brings out the simplicity of our relationship with God. Tim helps us see that when we come to God just as a child comes to a loving and caring father, that childlike prayer relationship develops intimacy with God. He shows us that intimacy with God enlarges and deepens our capacity for intimacy with others. That same intimacy with God removes rebellion from our hearts and enables us to surrender and trust in the One who loves us with an everlasting love and has our best interests at heart. Tim explains how our prayers reveal our belief system when it comes to trust. Reading this book, you will be reminded that prayer isn't about trying to look spiritually mature. However, prayer is about living in relationship with God where you talk to Him and He talks to you and He gives you all that you need while here on this earth to fulfill His will.

—Sharon Daugherty
Pastor, Victory Christian Center
Tulsa, Oklahoma

40 Days Through the Prayers of Jesus is a clear and powerful book. Basing it on the life of our Lord, Tim Cameron travels deeply into the prayers of Jesus. Following His perfect example, you will be drawn into a deeper relationship with God and intercession for others. Every page in the book is an invitation to be more like Him. You will not end the book the same person you started.

—JOHN MASON
BEST-SELLING AUTHOR OF *AN ENEMY CALLED AVERAGE*
NOTED SPEAKER AND EXECUTIVE AUTHOR COACH

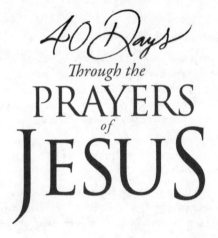

40 Days
Through the
PRAYERS
of
JESUS

TIM CAMERON

CHARISMA
HOUSE

Most Charisma House Book Group products are available at special quantity discounts for bulk purchase for sales promotions, premiums, fund-raising, and educational needs. For details, write Charisma House Book Group, 600 Rinehart Road, Lake Mary, Florida 32746, or telephone (407) 333-0600.

40 Days Through the Prayers of Jesus by Tim Cameron
Published by Charisma House
Charisma Media/Charisma House Book Group
600 Rinehart Road
Lake Mary, Florida 32746
www.charismahouse.com

Cover design by Lisa Rae McClure
Design Director: Justin Evans

Visit the author's website at timcameronprayer.com.

Library of Congress Cataloging-in-Publication Data:
An application to register this book for cataloging has been submitted to the Library of Congress.
International Standard Book Number: 978-1-62999-165-8
E-book ISBN: 978-1-62999-166-5

17 18 19 20 21 — 7 6 5 4 3 2 1
Printed in the United States of America

I dedicate this book to these people whose dedication to prayer has been my inspiration: Bill Sanders, Lattie McDonough, Dr. Mike Henderson, Joe Mooberry, Aunt Joanne, and my precious wife, Annamae.

Also, to those "Hall of Famers" of prayer, whose writings have provoked so many to pray, including me: Leonard Ravenhill, Andrew Murray, E. Stanley Jones, Rees Howells, Sylvia Gunter, Oswald Chambers, and E. M. Bounds.

CONTENTS

INTRODUCTION

FOR DECADES TEACHERS have used the saying "There are three great methods of teaching: example, example, and example." There is no greater model of a life of prayer than Jesus's journey. I am inviting you to take an expedition for forty days and travel deeply into the prayers of Jesus, savor them, and let them saturate your soul. From His first recorded prayer at the baptism by John to the last time He prayed as He ascended to heaven, you will understand what Christ's prayer life teaches and correspondingly yearn to invite it to penetrate all that is you.

What Christian doesn't want to be more effective in prayer? Who would disagree with the importance of prayer in the life of a Christ follower? It would be like saying you really don't need to read and study your Bible that much. Prayer and the Word are the staples of life in Christ. Yet it seems so few Christians experience the purpose of prayer: first, intimacy with Christ, and then the power to call down His blessings on others.

As you journey through this book, you will go to school and receive new, provoking, and insightful instruction from the master Teacher on prayer. The Holy Spirit will lead you to a place of intimacy with Christ that you long for, and you will begin to see more answers to your prayers. Are you stuck in a lethargic, boring prayer routine? Then brace yourself. You are about to be launched into a higher realm. You are going to be taught by the greatest Teacher on prayer. You will understand and taste the life and vibrancy that can be found in prayer.

I am challenging you to take a forty-day journey of simplicity. Simply dive deep into His prayers. Soak in the anointing oil of the spirit of prayer that resides in His examples. Look directly into Jesus's prayer life and let Him tutor you. But steel yourself, for as the Teacher He will instruct, reprove, and correct. Can you embrace this and invite His teaching profoundly into your mind, emotions, and will?

Obviously this little work does not answer all the questions about prayer. No library would have space to chronicle the volumes that could be written on the mysteries of prayer. Only Jesus has the final word on prayer. However, tethering ourselves to Jesus's example will pull and simultaneously entice us into the spirit of prayer that was His reality.

You are putting an instrument in your hands that will open a portal for you to be personally mentored by the most knowledgeable and powerful Teacher on prayer in the universe, the Lord Jesus Christ. He gave specific instructions to His disciples on prayer as He lived among them for three short years. He did this because prayer was His passion. He wants to give you His personal counsel in prayer. He wants it to be your life's passion.

Prayer was His direct line to speak to and listen to the Father. It was His first thought and practice when He woke. It guided every word and action of His life. Prayer was His vision for His followers, both individuals and the church as a whole. When almost everyone was arguing and contemplating, "Who is this man?," His passion for prayer answered the question. In John 2:17 as Jesus cleared the temple, the disciples remembered the snapshot of the Messiah in Psalm

69:9: "For the zeal of Your house has consumed me, and the insults of those who insulted You fell on me." His zeal was for His house to be a house of prayer.

My life came to a messy, grinding halt some years ago with a failed major surgery that required more and more major surgery and left me with a debilitating pain syndrome and in and out of a wheelchair. I labored for years with constant chronic pain, pain crises, panic attacks, and insomnia resulting from pain. In the throes of this pain I recalled a promise I had made myself, "Before I enter the kingdom of heaven, I will know what it means to pray and to often see answers to prayer."

It was in this backdrop that I set out to study everything I could get my hands on about prayer in the life of the believer. After devouring many books, I remained stuck in a stagnant, powerless prayer life. It was then that I decided to see what Christ's prayers would teach me. Following His example from the Gospels has led me to see miraculous, breathtaking answers to prayer. In humility and brokenness I confess the Holy Spirit has allowed me to call down God's blessing on people hundreds of miles away, sometimes immediately. And honestly, there is absolutely nothing special about me. A cursory examination of my entire life would leave me disqualified. There lies part of the unearthing of praying the way Jesus prays—all things are possible with Him.

In this book you will discover many of the secrets, mysteries, and provoking lessons His prayer life teaches. You will read real-life stories that support the truth: we can know Him intimately and have *daily* answers to prayer. The awesome answers to our prayers can be the testimony of our lives.

I must offer one caveat regarding prayer: prayer is not the

goal—intimacy with Jesus is. Any thought of achieving a life of prayer that is characterized by more and more prayer and answers to prayer is sheer vanity and futility unless it ushers us into deeper intimacy with God.

Dare to take this journey with me. At times your thinking might be scandalized and your propriety challenged, but you will be provoked to pray.

So why forty days? The number forty is significant in the Scriptures, particularly with the life of Jesus. The number forty is associated with new beginnings, testing, and victory in battles you would usually lose. When God wanted to bring transformation, often the process lasted forty days. It rained forty days and forty nights during the Flood, and Noah and his family remained in the ark another forty days while the water receded. When they were finally able to leave the ark, the world was different, new, and they were on the precipice of a new beginning.

The giant Goliath taunted the army of Israel for forty days, morning and evening. But then David, who was only a young shepherd, took a stand against the giant who dared to "defy the armies of the living God" (1 Sam. 17:26). After his legendary defeat of Goliath David was no longer viewed as merely a shepherd; he had become a mighty warrior and man of valor, and he eventually became king of Israel.[1]

More importantly Jesus fasted for forty days (Luke 4:2) following the first time He prayed in public at His baptism. While lifting His hands and blessing the disciples, He ascended to heaven forty days after His resurrection (Luke 24:50; Acts 1:3). Forty days in the prayers of Jesus can change your life.

DAY 1

EVERYTHING BEGINS
WITH PRAYER

Now when all the people were baptized, and when Jesus also had been baptized and was praying, the heavens were opened, and the Holy Spirit descended in a bodily form like a dove on Him, and a voice came from heaven which said, "You are My beloved Son. In You I am well pleased."
—LUKE 3:21–22

THE MAGNIFICENT OPPORTUNITY looms before us—our lives can be dramatically changed by the power of Jesus Christ, being conformed to His image and transformed by the renewing of our minds (Rom. 8:29; 12:1–2). We can experience the victorious Christian life for ourselves and see victories in the lives of others as well. Yet there is greater significance to be realized—we can bring glory to God and build His kingdom. All of this begins with and is maintained by prayer.

Understanding this, Jesus gave us a visible, audible, and miraculous example of the importance of prayer. At the very beginning He began with prayer. Jesus prayed while He was being baptized. Then He immediately went to the desert for forty days of fasting, which was obviously accompanied by prayer. Jesus prayed about all things as He navigated life, and He stole away often to pray and listen to the Father. Prayer is how Jesus began His public life, and it is how He wants us to begin all things in our lives.

LIFE'S FOUNDATION

It didn't matter if the issue at hand was profound or an everyday incident—Jesus began all things with prayer. Before setting out to preach and cast out demons throughout Galilee, He rose a great while before sunrise to pray (Mark 1:35–39). When they rolled the stone away from Lazarus's tomb, Jesus prayed for all to hear before raising him from the dead (John 11:40–44). And as He sat at a table for dinner with two disciples on the road to Emmaus, He simply prayed (Luke 24:30–31). Jesus's example leads us to pray before taking that new job, before a proposal of marriage, and on the way to work every morning.

Beginning all things in prayer is a foundational discipline of the Christian life. The times of praying in stillness and solitude are when God reaches into our minds, emotions, and wills, the deepest places of our souls. In the quietness of prayer we free ourselves from the constant distractions of the world and the nagging whispers of our past, dysfunctions, and sins. Beginning all things in prayer during the day and having close and continual fellowship in prayer with God will leave its mark on us.

As we follow our Lord by beginning everything in prayer, we position ourselves to receive the glorious benefits that flow from this way of living. First and foremost, prayer is our path to intimacy with God. There is no other way to deeply know God apart from the stillness of prayer.

> Be still and know that I am God; I will be exalted among the nations, I will be exalted in the earth.
>
> —Psalm 46:10

In the quiet stillness of prayer we answer God's invitation to spend time with Him, discover His nature, and become intimately acquainted with Him.

SPIRITUAL TRAINING

One of the sweetest and most powerful benefits of beginning all things in prayer is that our "spiritual ears" will be trained to recognize His voice. We learn to quiet our thoughts, our educational training, and our persuasions. We become deaf to anything except His voice and will. By following Christ's example and beginning all things in prayer, we are able to discern His voice above the cacophony of the world and the murmurs of the enemy. Learning to recognize His voice is fundamental preparation for hearing the Lord through the Word.

Beginning all things with prayer leads to right hearing. Right hearing produces right speaking. This is how we learn to speak words of life to people, to speak the language of the kingdom, and to call people to their destiny in Christ. Many of us desire to have the tongue of a disciple, of one who is taught or learned:

> The Lord God has given me the tongue of the learned, that
> I may know how to sustain him who is weary with a word;
> He awakens me morning by morning; He awakens my ear
> to listen as the learned.
>
> —Isaiah 50:4

Jesus learned to speak a word in season to the weary by being awakened morning by morning and having God open His ears to hear. It can be the same with us.

THE FULLNESS OF THE HOLY SPIRIT IN US

The foundation of any relationship is trust. Trust is a by-product of knowing someone deeply. When we begin all things in prayer, our relationship with God goes deeper and deeper. We will find ourselves easily trusting Him with events that may have sent shockwaves through our lives in times past. Trust strengthens our faith, and we begin the great transformation to become childlike again. With faith like a child we trust the One we know loves us deeply and sacrificed so much on our behalf.

Jesus Christ left us the example of beginning all things in prayer at His baptism. As He prayed, the heavens opened, and the Holy Spirit descended on the fully human Jesus and filled Him. This is what happened to Jesus. This is also the great promise to us. By beginning all things in prayer, we open ourselves to the fullness of the Holy Spirit and His power. The Holy Spirit will help us in our lack and intercede for us. What an amazing thought! The Holy Spirit will teach us to pray. He will strengthen us in our resolve to begin all things in prayer. The Holy Spirit will perfect our prayers even in our weakness.

The natural, spiritual outcome of being filled with the fullness of the Holy Spirit will begin to take place in our lives—we will take up the mantle to fulfill Christ's prayer: "Your kingdom come; Your will be done on earth, as it is in heaven" (Matt. 6:10). We will become intercessors.

Can you see the scene now—John the Baptist baptizing Christ while He is praying. The Holy Spirit descends in bodily form like a dove, and an audible voice is heard from heaven. What must those gathered around have thought? God declared to the world in front of many people that Jesus is the Son of God, in whom He is well pleased. The word must have spread like wildfire.

In the midst of all this the lesson is clear for us—Jesus began everything in His life of ministry with prayer.

WHEN YOU PRAY

All things should begin with prayer.

What are one or two steps you can take today to establish a lifestyle of beginning all things with prayer?

1) Begin my devotions with prayer, then
2) Continue my day with prayer

Psalm 91
Psalm 23
Psalm 121
Psalm 138

PRAYER OPENS UP COMMUNICATION WITH GOD

Now when all the people were baptized, and when Jesus also had been baptized and was praying, the heavens were opened, and the Holy Spirit descended in a bodily form like a dove on Him, and a voice came from heaven which said, "You are My beloved Son. In You I am well pleased."
—LUKE 3:21–22

I T IS MUCH more than coincidence that while Jesus was praying, the Holy Spirit descended upon Him. Luke allowed us to see the integral place that prayer was going to play in the life of the Savior, and rightly so. Just as we do, Jesus needed all the benefits that prayer can bring. Christ's baptism was His first public appearance as an adult, and prayer was a key component. At His baptism He began a practice that continued throughout His life: He prayed about all things.

THE HEAVENS OPENED

It was prayer that opened up the heavens—yes, even for Jesus. Prayer creates a stream of communication between God and man. Christ was modeling what He would later say to the disciples: "Therefore pray in this manner: Our Father who is in heaven, hallowed be Your name" (Matt. 6:9). We can communicate with our Lord in many ways—through worship, giving, and acts of service, to name some of the most obvious; however, we will never know our Lord and Savior intimately if we do not learn to pray. Prayer is the key to approach and open heaven's doorway.

The Bible is replete with instances in which men and women prayed and heard directly from God. And the answers to those prayers were as varied as the encounters we face daily. Hannah was heartbroken because she could not conceive a child. To compound Hannah's despair, a rival mocked and tormented her. She cried out to the Lord and her prayer was answered. (See 1 Samuel 1.) Her son Samuel became one of the great prophets of Israel.

Jehoshaphat faced an overwhelming enemy who was bent on his destruction. In his own hopelessness he cried out to God and uttered the phrase that is all too familiar to us: "We do not know what we should do" (2 Chron. 20:12). The Lord answered Jehoshaphat's prayer and told him, "Do not fear, nor be dismayed because of this great army, for the battle is not yours, but God's" (v. 15). The Lord gave him a strategy that defied all logic. Jehoshaphat appointed singers for the Lord and those praising Him. When they began singing and praising, God set ambushes against the enemy. Jehoshaphat's enemies were defeated without the armies of Judah having to fight; all they did was worship. (See 2 Chronicles 20:22–30.)

The blind man Bartimaeus uttered a simple request in response to Jesus's question: "What do you want Me to do for you?" The blind man said, "Rabbi, that I might receive my sight" (Mark 10:51). Bartimaeus was immediately healed.

The Gospels record three times that the Father spoke from heaven to Jesus and others heard it: at Jesus's baptism in Luke 3:21–22, at the transfiguration in Luke 9:28–36, and for a crowd of Greeks in John 12:28. Each of these times when the Father spoke audibly to Jesus so that others could hear His words, Jesus was in the act of praying. It is meant to be the same for us. Prayer is when we speak to our Father in heaven and expect to hear an answer. We must believe that the Lord takes great delight in answering the prayers of His children.

> Now I know that the LORD saves His anointed; He will answer him from His holy heaven with the saving strength of His right hand.
>
> —PSALM 20:6

The first step to victory in spiritual warfare is to trust and believe that the Lord hears our prayers. We have made the Lord our hope and praise. In every challenge with the world and the spiritual forces of darkness we must call on the name of Jesus and on His Spirit to open up the heavens and empower us.

EXPERIENCING THE FULLNESS OF GOD IN PRAYER

While Jesus was praying, the Holy Spirit descended like a dove and landed on Him and the Father spoke to the Son. Here we see the majestic mystery of the Trinity: the Father, the Son, and the Holy Spirit. In prayer we have the rich opportunity to experience the fullness of God in our lives, including unique aspects of the Trinity: the blessing of the Father, the mind of Christ, and the inspiration of the Holy Spirit.

The blessing of the Father

Christ received the blessing of the Father at His baptism. It was through prayer that Christ obtained this glorious expression of the Father's love and approval. In this one event the truth was revealed to all who heard: "You are My beloved Son. In You I am well pleased" (Luke 3:22). In this one prayer we get a glimpse into the mind of God. We get a glimpse of the Trinity and the enigmatic unity of the Father, Son, and Holy Spirit. We see the Father's love for the Son.

A father's blessing is powerful and has profound meaning. At Jesus's baptism the Father openly spoke the most perfect words any son can hear—words of identification, approval, and blessing. Jesus was told He was the beloved Son of God and the Father was well pleased with His actions as a man.

The Father's blessing includes words of encouragement and can even include prophetic words concerning the future (Ps. 21:2–6). The blessing of the Father is the ultimate act of affirmation. It catapults the recipient into God's purposes for his or her life. Ephesians tells us that the Father "has blessed us with every spiritual blessing....He chose us in Him before the foundation of the world, to be holy and blameless before Him in love; He predestined us to adoption as sons to Himself through Jesus Christ according to the good pleasure of His will....In Him we have redemption through His blood and the forgiveness of sins according to the riches of His grace" (Eph. 1:3–7). But it doesn't end there—the blessing of the Father includes the promise of the Holy Spirit being poured out on future generations (Isa. 44:1–5). Christ came to fulfill the law, not destroy it (Matt. 5:17), so all who follow Him receive the Father's blessing.

The Father's blessing of Jesus started at His baptism; it thrust Him into God's plans for His life. And just as the Father blessed Jesus, He blesses you. As a follower of Christ, you have been adopted into God's family. The Father blesses you with every blessing in heavenly places. He blesses you to be a blessing. He promises to hear your prayers. He bestows all the rights of His kingdom to you as you follow Him, and you can minister that blessing to others and your offspring.

The mind of Christ

It is God's will that we not be conformed to this world. Rather, He wants us to be transformed in our minds (Rom. 12:1–2). Our thoughts are not in a vacuum; they produce the actions that come from us. We must strive to bring every thought into captivity to the obedience of Christ (2 Cor. 10:5). Paul wrote to the Philippians, "Let this mind be in you all, which was also in Christ Jesus" (Phil. 2:5). Changing our deepest thought patterns, false identities, strongholds, addictions, and all other obstacles embedded in our minds is only accomplished as we experience His fullness through prayer. Change that produces new thoughts, ones that are in agreement with His thoughts, requires us to behold the Lord daily and abide in His presence.

It is in the depths of solitary prayer, praying the Word, and constant prayer through the day that we begin to think the thoughts of Christ and our minds are renewed. Renewing our minds is a battle. Ephesians 6:10–18 speaks of the armor that we need for the battle. The Word of God is the only weapon identified (v. 17). But Paul uses the plural *weapons* when identifying the weapons of our warfare that pull down strongholds, cast down imaginations, and bring every thought into captivity to the obedience of Christ (2 Cor. 10:4–5). I believe Paul identifies an additional weapon in Ephesians 6:18: "Pray in the Spirit always with all kinds of prayer and supplication." The weapons of our warfare in the renewal of our minds are the Word of God and Spirit-filled prayer.

The inspiration of the Spirit

Our experience with the fullness of the Holy Spirit is governed by this one guiding principle: God gives the Holy Spirit. He gives all of the Spirit's truth and inspiration in response to our prayers. Jesus received the Holy Spirit while He prayed and yielded Himself in baptism. Being inspired by the Holy Spirit, He was led into the wilderness. The Spirit led Jesus all through His life. The Spirit came to the disciples as they met together and prayed. The Holy Spirit was given to them as the inspiration and guide into all truth (John 16:13).

Paul teaches us that the Holy Spirit is meant for everyone, every day of our lives: "But *be filled* with the Spirit. Speak to one another in psalms, hymns, and spiritual songs, singing and making melody in your heart to the Lord" (Eph. 5:18–19, emphasis added). The idea behind *be filled* is to be constantly and continuously filled. Prayer is the place we ask for this continual filling. And we have this promise: "If you then, being evil, know how to give good gifts to your children, how much more will your heavenly Father give the Holy Spirit to those who ask Him?" (Luke 11:13).

It is crucial for our maturity as sons and daughters to look to the Holy Spirit every day—to call out to Him in the morning hours, seek His guidance during the day, and be cognizant of His presence with us. He will warn us when we are missing God's truth in any situation (John 16:13). The effectual work of the Holy Spirit will energize our prayers with power and strengthen us to persevere in our requests for all the saints (Eph. 6:18). The Holy Spirit will equip us with His gifts to do the work of the ministry (Rom. 12:6–8). If we submit to the anointing of the Holy Spirit, He will take us far beyond what we are capable of in the natural; He will teach us what no man or book can reveal (1 John 2:20, 27). The Holy Spirit will anoint us to set captives free and speak words of edification, exhortation, and comfort to God's people (Isa. 61:1–3; 1 Cor. 14:1–3).

If we want all that the Holy Spirit has for us, we must learn to ask in prayer, and often.

When You Pray

It is through the Holy Spirit and prayer that you hear from the Father.

① How have you experienced the blessing of the Father? ② Can you think of a time when you knew you had the mind of Christ when making a decision? ③ How have you experienced the inspiration of the Holy Spirit?

④ How do you hear from the Holy Spirit?

For further study see John 14:16–21; 1 Corinthians 12:4–6; Ephesians 4:4–6; Hebrews 3:7–11.

① I have been healed, I have divine health, protection & prosperity • ② Doing a second work scan ③ my french unit false church - interpreting, proofreading, etc. ④ a leap inside me.

DAY 3

PRAYER IS A PRIORITY

*In the morning, rising up a great while before sunrise, He went
out and departed to a solitary place. And there He prayed. Simon
and those who were with Him followed Him, and when they found
Him, they said to Him, "Everyone is searching for You."* [1]
—MARK 1:35–37

THE NEWS ABOUT Jesus was spreading over the whole
region of Galilee. Galilee was a large province with more
than twenty towns. What Jesus was doing and saying was
like nothing people had seen or heard before. Jesus went into
the synagogue on the Sabbath at Capernaum and taught
with an authority that let everyone know He was not just
another teacher of the law. This was not business as usual.
The people were amazed and astonished. He cast out demons
and healed the sick there that same day.

The word spread quickly, and later that night the whole town
came to where He was. Yes, the whole town of Capernaum
(population estimated to be between 1,000 and 1,500 people
at the time[2]) gathered at the doorstep, bringing the sick and
demon-possessed and clamoring for Jesus (Mark 1:32–34).

Can you picture the scene? Can you see yourself there?
Imagine the sense of anticipation, the stirring of the people,
the talk, and the electricity in the air. This was a dramatically taxing, emotionally draining, and physically demanding
day for Christ the man.

What did Jesus do the next morning? Did He get caught
up on His much-needed sleep? Perhaps take a late breakfast?

No. He began a pattern that is referenced many times by the Gospels. In fact, as Luke observed, "Jesus often withdrew to lonely places and prayed" (Luke 5:16, NIV).

MAKING PRAYER A PRIORITY

Christ was a man; He was human. Yet despite His humanness He consistently made prayer a priority in His life. John tells us pointedly that Jesus "became flesh and dwelt among us, and we saw His glory, the glory as the only Son of the Father, full of grace and truth" (John 1:14). Jesus was as human as you and I are.

+ He was tired. "Suddenly a great storm arose on the sea, so that the boat was covered with the waves. But He was asleep" (Matt. 8:24). "As they sailed, He fell asleep" (Luke 8:23).

+ He was thirsty. "After this, Jesus, knowing that everything was now accomplished, that the Scripture might be fulfilled, said, 'I thirst'" (John 19:28).

+ He was hungry. "And He had fasted for forty days and forty nights, and then He was hungry" (Matt. 4:2).

So when we look at the scene in Capernaum, we must acknowledge Jesus's humanness. Even though His fatiguing schedule from the previous day had included preaching during the day and working miracles late into the evening, Jesus still rose very early to pray. It is easier for us to think of Christ in the divine sense rather than the human realm. We don't usually consider that Christ was hungry, thirsty, or in need of rest, but He was. Think about the grueling schedule He must have kept and that He often got little sleep. Yet according to Mark 1:35, He rose "a great while before sunrise" or "very early in the morning" (NIV) to pray.

For fifteen years of my married life I rose at 3:45 a.m. seven days a week to deliver newspapers before heading off to work. For the first few years of this craziness I walked around sleep deprived, yawning in meetings during the day and barely able to function. Every time I got a few free minutes, I disappeared somewhere and took a power nap. Jesus had this habit of stealing away too, but with Him it was to pray. Jesus was teaching and healing the sick late into the evening. He was sharing His life with the disciples 24/7. The crowds were pressing in on Him. Yet He chose to make prayer a priority.

EARLY WILL I SEEK YOU

Jesus was always teaching the disciples. He took every opportunity to share parables and instruct them. By seeking time with the Father in prayer at the start of the day, He was sending a clear message that the morning is the best time for prayer and intercession. In the morning our spirits are fresh and our minds are uncluttered by the pressures of the day to come. Oh, we have so many pressures. Our lives can become a tangled mess of appointments, meetings, errands, telephone calls, expectations, and commitments.

We are nearing "technology overload." We are addicted. What began as a convenient way to communicate has turned into a compulsive need to check texts, return e-mails, and feel that rush from social media. Is your smartphone the last thing you touch at night and the first thing you reach for in morning?

Mark noted that Jesus went to a solitary place. Our addiction to stimulation is a dramatic distraction from prayer and a life of intimacy with Jesus. For Jesus the place to pray was a solitary place, a place away from the noise and commotion of people and the world, a place where He could be quiet and listen to the Father. It must be the same for us. At some point we have to turn off the phone if we want to receive His call.

Jesus set the example of starting the day in prayer, taking time with the Father before facing the day. Despite the crowds, the demands put on Him, and even His own personal needs, He still prayed. Amongst our pressures, the expectations of others, and the assault of information, can we make time to pray? Can we follow Jesus's example and seek God in the morning? Is it our hearts' cry to spend time with God? Can we make starting the day with prayer a priority? The health of our spiritual lives and souls depends on prayer. Let our actions mirror the cry of the psalmist: "O God, You are my God; early will I seek you; my soul thirsts for You, my flesh faints for You, in a dry and thirsty land with no water" (Ps. 63:1).

WHEN YOU PRAY

No matter what happens, you need to make prayer a priority.

What are two of the greatest pressures you face daily that keep you from praying?

What can you do about them?

What practical steps can you take to make prayer a priority?

① Getting things done — my list.

② Reset my priorities

③ Have my devotion ins upstairs
I do devotions & pray lot, then
exercises & iphone before
getting out of bed

DAY 4

THE SECRET PLACE

In the morning, rising up a great while before sunrise, He went out and departed to a solitary place. And there He prayed. Simon and those who were with Him followed Him, and when they found Him, they said to Him, "Everyone is searching for You." [1]
—MARK 1:35–37

WHERE DO YOU pray? Is where you pray really that important? Evidently it is; Jesus specifically mentioned where we should and shouldn't pray.

Where not to pray: in a location chosen so you can be seen by others. "When you pray, you shall not be like the hypocrites. For they love to pray standing in the synagogues and on the street corners that they may be seen by men. Truly I say to you, they have their reward" (Matt. 6:5).

Where to pray: in private in your room. "But you, when you pray, enter your closet, and when you have shut your door, pray to your Father who is in secret. And your Father who sees in secret will reward you openly" (v. 6).

While Jesus was in Capernaum, Mark indicated that Simon and his companions went to look for Jesus. When they found Him, they exclaimed, "Everyone is searching for You" (Mark 1:37). Mark paints the picture that Jesus went away in seclusion to pray and that everyone was trying to find Him. Obviously He didn't stay close, and He wasn't easy to find.

As previously discussed, Jesus was teaching the disciples by example. He not only demonstrated when to pray but also where to pray. Although later Jesus will address these issues pointedly with the disciples, for now He let His example teach. I wonder if they perceived it. Pray early. Pray in secret. Pray to your Father in heaven. Pray not to be heard by man but by your Father, who is in secret.

The Secret to Prayer

This is a great secret to prayer: *pray in secret*. Prayer is meant for the Father; we don't pray to be heard by men.

Most Christians have heard the term or some variation their entire Christian lives: *quiet time*. Various denominations and movements call it other things: daily devotional, seven-minute quiet time, morning watch, and so on. All of these refer to the same precept, coming to the Lord in the early morning, seeking Him, and committing our day to Him in prayer. It is the spiritual discipline of communing with the Lord. The names of daily devotionals meant to encourage us in this communion are so familiar. Just hearing their titles conjures up memories of seeking and finding the Lord in the early morning hours: *My Utmost for His Highest, Jesus Calling, Streams in the Desert, The Book of Common Prayer,* and so many more.

We see this pattern of the Lord's early-morning prayer beginning at the start of His ministry. He repeatedly departed to a solitary place, either in the hills, out of town, or in a remote garden. There He found a place where there were no distractions. There He showed us the power of prayer in a secret place.

The Word of God gives us clear evidence that men and women who want to be used of God must know what it is to encounter the Lord and be in His presence.

- Abraham: "Now Abraham got up early in the morning and went to the place where he stood before the LORD" (Gen. 19:27).

- Moses: "The LORD spoke to Moses face to face, just as a man speaks to his friend" (Exod. 33:11).

- Joshua: "When [Moses] returned to the camp, his servant Joshua, the son of Nun, a young man, did not depart from the tent [of meeting]" (Exod. 33:11).

- Isaiah: "With my soul I have desired You in the night, Yes, by my spirit within me I will seek You early" (Isa. 26:9, NKJV).

- David: "O LORD, in the morning You will hear my voice; in the morning I will direct my prayer to You, and I will watch expectantly" (Ps. 5:3).

THE BENEFITS OF THE SECRET PLACE

Jesus told the disciples to come away to a remote place and rest awhile (Mark 6:31). He went with them, and they fellowshipped together there. Of all the many magnificent benefits of being in the secret place with God, none is more precious than simply being in His presence, experiencing intimacy with the Creator. Our repeated trips to the place of solitude, the secret place, result in an unfolding revelation of Jesus Christ in our hearts. Our Lord may grant us many blessings and answers to prayer, but it is in the secret place that He bestows on us the greatest gift He can give: His very presence.

The marvelous truth about the secret place is it is not so secret. And we all are eligible for entrance. It requires but two things from us to enter: time and a love for Jesus. Put these two together, and we are given an opportunity to gain understanding into the nature of God. Jesus said, "He who has My commandments and keeps them is the one who loves Me. And he who loves Me will be loved by My Father. And I will love him and will reveal Myself to him" (John 14:21).

For a moment, right now, take a deep breath and meditate on the enormity of what Jesus speaks to us. "If a man loves Me, he will keep My word. My Father will love him, and We will come to him, and make Our home with him" (v. 23). Did you see and feel that word *We*? The eternal God, three in one, will meet us in the secret place.

We live in turbulent and violent times. Uncertainty seems to loom around every corner. Raising children, working, challenges in relationships, and our quest for unity in our Christian fellowship are all under assault from the world. Yet the Lord has made provision for us in this tempest. God's Word provides a way for us. He entreats us to enter the refuge where His watchfulness leads us to a place of safety.

> He who dwells in the shelter of the Most High shall abide under the shadow of the Almighty. I will say of the LORD, "He is my refuge and my fortress, my God in whom I trust." Surely He shall deliver you from the snare of the hunter and from the deadly pestilence. He shall cover you with His feathers, and under His wings you shall find protection; His faithfulness shall be your shield and wall.
>
> —PSALM 91:1–4

None of us are immune from times when we are consumed or seemingly engulfed with pain and sorrow. The attacks of the enemy can seem relentless. Yet even in the midst of this onslaught Christ has reserved a secret place for us, where the shaking cannot move us.

For in the time of trouble He will hide me in His pavilion; in the shelter of His tabernacle He will hide me; He will set me up on a rock. Now my head will be lifted up above my enemies encircling me; therefore I will offer sacrifices of joy in His tabernacle; I will sing, yes, I will sing praises to the LORD.
—PSALM 27:5–6

In all the craziness and chaos of life Christ invites us to a different place, a habitation of rest. This secret place is a location unknown to the world and impenetrable to its carnage. Jesus is calling you. Can you hear Him with your spirit? "Come to Me, all you who labor and are heavily burdened, and I will give you rest" (Matt. 11:28).

The secret place is the place of answered prayer. It is where we learn to pray according to His will. It is the place where we learn to hear. "If you remain in Me, and My words remain in you, you will ask whatever you desire, and it shall be done for you" (John 15:7).

WHEN YOU PRAY

God wants to meet you in a special, secret place.

Do you have a consistent place that you go to pray? Where is it?

If the answer to the first question is no, then give prayerful thought to a place where you could pray daily.

_____

_____

_____

_____

DAY 5

CHOOSING BETWEEN GOOD AND BEST

*Yet even more so His fame went everywhere. And great crowds
came together to hear and to be healed by Him of their infir-
mities. But He withdrew to the wilderness and prayed.*[1]
—LUKE 5:15–16

THE ENEMY OF the best is always the good." That's what
one of my mentors, Dr. Charles Farah, would say. People
who are popular will have many others pulling at them.
Anyone with multiple responsibilities will daily face the
decision to leave something undone.

WHAT COMES FIRST?

What is the most important decision you will make every
day? Is it what suit or outfit to put on? What engagement to
say no to? Which calls to return? How to prioritize the many
tasks pulling at your limited time? Or is it the decision to
spend time with the Lord and pray the first thing in the day?

In my training as a school superintendent one of the last
exercises every new applicant faced was the "in-box" test. The
challenge was to take an in-box of ten items and prioritize
them by importance, deciding which you would tackle first
that day and which could wait to be addressed later. I learned
that invariably, disguised in the ten items, there was always
a safety item that was difficult to identify. A safety item is
something related to the safety of students, staff, or patrons.

Safety items always take priority above every other administrative task. And it is the same way in our spiritual lives. The safety item for our relationship with Christ is having time alone with Him every day, preferably at the start of the day, in prayer and the Word.

SYMMETRY

There is a great contrast in Christ's public and private life. His public life was one filled with great crowds, the power of the Spirit in operation, and teaching with authority. His private life was one of solitude, prayer, and listening to the Father. How does your private life match up to your public life? Is there symmetry between the two?

My pastor is a man full of the grace and mercy of the Lord. He is known for being gracious in his dealings with others. He is not perfect; he makes mistakes like any of us. Our church had been working on a project, and I felt he had missed a point of information that would have helped make a better decision. I really felt like he needed to know what he had missed as it was important, but who wants to suggest a word of correction to your pastor? After much prayer I decided to make him aware of his misstep. His reaction was totally predictable. His immediate response was, "What do we need to do to correct my mistake? How can we make sure this doesn't happen again?" A few weeks later I listened as my pastor revealed he has been fasting and praying every Monday for fifteen years. This one statement told me a great deal about my pastor's private life. I have seen his public life, and believe me, his private life and public life are in symmetry with Christ. And as I always say, "You can tell everything about where a person stands spiritually by how he or she receives instruction or correction, no matter how gently suggested or given."

Jesus prayed to His Father—we know that. He prayed for His disciples. Because He was a man, He likely prayed for Himself, that He might be strengthened for service. The lesson Jesus teaches us is so clear. Prayer was His daily priority. He understood the need for time in the secret place to hear from the Father to start the day.

His life and the Word teach us about prayer. The teaching is so simple and clear: "He went out and departed to a solitary place. And there He prayed" and "He withdrew to the wilderness and prayed" (Mark 1:35; Luke 5:16). Jesus chose the best over the good.

The question of the hour is: Do you pray? I don't mean a quick blessing at the dinner table, a traditional good night prayer with your spouse or a child, or a rote prayer at church as the pastor leads the congregation. I mean do you have a consistent place where you go daily to wait on the Lord? A place where you speak to Him and He speaks to you? A place where you are still and look deeply into the Lord as He looks into you? Are you intimate with the Lord in prayer daily? Is your public life a reflection of choosing the best in your private life?

LORD OF MY HABITS

One translation of Luke 5:16 states, "Jesus often withdrew to lonely places and prayed" (NIV). The key word in this text is *often*. The ISV says, "However, he continued his habit of retiring to deserted places and praying." He made it a habit to go away and pray—He did it often. No matter how busy it seemed, no matter how many people were clamoring for His attention,

He often withdrew. It was His practice. If Jesus, the Son of God, the Word made flesh, made it His practice to find some time alone to pray, how much more should we make it ours?

What are your habits? A habit is something that is your custom or practice, and it can be especially hard to give up. One of the difficulties with forming a new habit is that we may be attempting to break old habits that have been formed over years and years. And all of us know that one of the raging conflicts we face in life is breaking bad habits and forming positive habits.

One morning in my quiet time before the Lord I heard Him as clearly as if words had been spoken: "It's time to put the newspaper down." I laughed out loud as I contemplated that thought. In delivering newspapers every morning for fifteen years, I developed the habit of finishing my routine by sitting down at a coffee shop and reading the paper for a few minutes. Now I had finally come to a place in my career where I didn't need to work a second job, but I still started the day the same way, newspaper in hand, sitting at the coffee shop. Now I could relax, enjoy the newspaper, and not be in a hurry. The newspaper was the first thing I meditated on every day. Reading the newspaper is not a bad thing—in fact, it is good to be informed about what is happening in the world around us. But reading the newspaper first was not what was best. It took me quite a while to break the newspaper habit, but I did break it. I replaced the newspaper habit with another habit—meditating on God's Word. I chose the best over the good, and for more than fifteen years I have devoured the Word of God habitually.

So I ask again: What are your habits? Are you choosing what is best, or are you merely choosing what is good?

LORD OF MY TIME

One of the great lessons of life and relationships is that there is no substitute for time. From friendships to marriage, you cannot cheat time. Dennis Jernigan, the great gospel song-writer, has stated that *intimacy* means "into me see."[2] In order to develop into-me-see intimacy, it takes time. In any relationship time is the vital element. No matter what excuses a person gives, no matter what a person says, show me how time is spent, and I will show you what is important to the person. How a person spends his or her time is a view into the soul.

Here is an even greater truth: there is no substitute for time alone with the Lord. A daily quiet time with God is a necessity for a relationship with the Lord. It is in our daily quiet time that we study the Bible, pray, and listen to the Lord. These practices bring life and vitality to our soul. But the morning watch or daily quiet time is not the goal. The goal is not to be so disciplined that we habitually have a quiet time with the Lord every morning for an hour. No, the goal of time with the Lord in the morning is to know Christ, have His presence in our life, and to be connected with Him throughout the entire day.

> And we know that the Son of God has come and has given us understanding, so that we may know Him who is true.
> —1 JOHN 5:20

As we spend time with Christ, His character will become our character. Our life will be hidden in His life, His nature will become our nature, and His habits will become our habits. (See Colossians 3:3; Ephesians 4:20–24; 2 Peter 1:3–5.) It is possible to become so intimately acquainted with a practice that you can do it without thinking. It becomes second nature, natural. When we find the secret place of abiding in Christ, when we make Him Lord of our time, our ordinary, daily interactions with people can move out of the realm of the mundane into the realm of the divinely appointed. They will be majestic opportunities to fulfill God's purposes. We will become fruitful Christians. All fruitfulness of this kind flows out of intimacy with Him.

There are two great hindrances to prayer. Listen carefully with your spirit. Revelation 3:6 states, "He who has an ear, let him hear what the Spirit says to the churches." The two great hindrances to prayer are busyness and worldliness. Busyness steals our time to pray, and worldliness diverts our will from prayer. People who are too busy to pray are too busy to live lives wholly given to Jesus. People who are too worldly to pray are living lives willfully given to the world, not to Jesus.

You cannot give to others what you do not possess yourself. It is truly in our private times of prayer and devotion that His presence increases within us. If your heart's desire is to influence others for Christ, to give hope to the hopeless, and to speak words of encouragement to the weary, then you must have the presence of the Lord in your life. There must be symmetry between your public life and your private life. You must learn to choose what is best. The presence of the Lord in your life is only attained by spending quiet time with Him; this is the one constant that must be in your life to call down God's blessings on others.

WHEN YOU PRAY

You must say no to good things to reserve time for the best.

Do you have any habits that use a significant amount of your time and don't benefit you spiritually? What are they?

What is the first step you can take to break those habits?

_____

_____

_____

_____

_____

_____

_____

_____

_____

_____

_____

_____

_____

_____

_____

_____

Day 6

ALL-NIGHT PRAYER

*In these days He went out to the mountain to pray and continued
all night in prayer to God. When it was day, He called for His disciples, and of them He chose twelve, whom He named apostles.*[1]
—Luke 6:12–13

The crowds were pressing in on Him. Hundreds, if not
thousands, showed up at the doorstep of the place where
He spent the night. He needed a place to pray with no inter-
ruptions. He had business to transact and needed to hear
from His Father about one of the most important decisions
He would make during His earthly time—the choosing
of the twelve disciples. So He headed to the mountains to
spend the night in prayer. A whole night!

Making Time for Prayer

It is incredible what we sometimes have to go through to just
carve out thirty minutes of prayer time—well, make that
fifteen minutes. In our way of thinking, an hour spent in
prayer would be a huge deal. We would qualify as spiritual
giants! But then we look at our Lord. He spent whole nights
in prayer, yet He was human, just like us, in every way. How
amazing and yet perplexing.

We have all these pressures, commitments, and requirements every day, and then there is the infamous to-do list. It
seems never-ending. Managing our time is a momentous task.
Today whole industries are built around assisting people in

29

planning and exercising conscious control over the amount of time spent on activities during the day. Productivity and outcomes are what we are after, what we are all about. Right?

There are two great differences in the way we see life and the way the Lord sees life.

Time

Time means everything to us. We squeeze it. We maximize it. We prioritize it. We cherish it. We try to figure how not to waste it, how to capitalize on it, and how to multiply it. But time means nothing to the Lord. He has all the time in the world. He is in no hurry. What He wants to accomplish in our lives can take forty minutes or forty years. He isn't concerned with the length of time it takes to accomplish His purposes. Hear these words with your spiritual ears: "You can't hurry the Spirit." If your goal is unbroken fellowship with the Lord in every minute of the day and if you want to secure Christ's presence to overcome each temptation that comes your way, then you must determine that spending time in the secret place every day is one of the great resolves of your life.

Open your spiritual eyes and read this carefully. There is something of much greater importance than all of our requests to the Lord for our personal needs and the needs of others for whom we intercede. There is a prerequisite to all of this—it is to have a deep, living relationship with the Father. He created us for this. He created us to commune with Him, delight in Him, and fulfill His will for our lives.

A great encumbrance to our relationship with the Lord is that we are preoccupied with other things. Instead of making everything secondary to the decision to spend time with the Lord every day, we hurriedly shove in a few minutes here and there with Him. We try to focus on the Lord for a few minutes while we scurry from one project to the other, from one appointment to the other, from one person to the next. Yet our example, Jesus, was willing to pray *all night*. Many of us might consider binge watching our favorite television show all night, but we would consider praying all night to be too extreme. Perhaps we should look again to our example. Perhaps we should ask God to stir up our hearts so that the thought of praying and spending time with Him all night is as appealing as watching our favorite television show.

Results

The short of it is that we want results. We want productivity. We have to see something tangible for our efforts. We transfer this fleshly propensity for the need to see results to our spiritual lives. We often don't see measurable results from our prayers, so we get discouraged and prayer wanes. The Lord simply does not measure our lives by our productivity. The Lord looks at all of our accomplishments, our degrees, and our projects-completed list, and He is not impressed. He doesn't manage by measurable outcomes. The Lord is out for depth in our relationship with Him. His goal is intimacy with us. He doesn't measure our lives by what is seen. He does His most significant work in the unseen. Our Lord wants His life deeply imbedded into the fabric of our souls. He wants our spirits exchanged for His, our character for His. "For the LORD sees not as man sees. For man looks on the outward appearance, but the LORD looks on the heart" (1 Sam. 16:7).

We need to consider the results of our prayers that are not measurable. Jesus knew that time spent in prayer was never a waste of time. Prayer produces results, even when we can't see them (2 Cor. 4:18). You might not receive the answer you wanted to a request (and sometimes you might not receive an answer at all), but the time spent in prayer still had the result of deepening your relationship with the Lord. Intimacy cannot be measured. And we can be confident that the end result of our time with Jesus will be a good one, because "He who has begun a good work in you will complete it" (Phil. 1:6, NKJV). When we put in the time, we can leave the results in the hands of the One who is working all things together for our good (Rom. 8:28).

AVAILABLE

I called up a long-time mentor recently to visit with him. When I asked him about a date the following week for us to get together for lunch, he responded that he wouldn't know for sure about his availability until the day before. That's all he said. It was awhile later until I remembered he rarely sets appointments in advance. His reason is that he always wants to be available to people he shepherds and those with immediate needs. One thing that is so unique about this man is his ability to focus on one person at a time. He is never hurried. He is available.

When I was a new Christian, I had the blessing to be discipled by a series of men, most of whom had a Navigators background. The Navigators is a ministry that advances the gospel throughout the world by discipleship—a call to discover life to the fullest in Christ. In its call to discipleship the Navigators place great importance on being faithful, available, and teachable. Availability is a huge issue in today's hectic, fast-paced culture. Just try to get a few Christians together to pray on a regular basis, and you will experience what great difficulty we have in putting first things first. Our busyness crowds out the most important things in life.

Jesus was available. Early in the morning, late at night, even all night, He made time available for prayer and for others. What about you? Are you available to others? Are you available to your fellowship or church? Are you available to the Lord?

WHEN YOU PRAY

Jesus was never in a hurry.

Do you have time for the Lord in your schedule?

Can you easily stop during the day and spend time with one person?

How do your goals and ambitions enrich your spiritual life?

Have you considered that the results of prayer are not always measurable?

_____

_____

_____

_____

_____

_____

_____

_____

DAY 7

THE KEY TO WISE DECISIONS

In these days He went out to the mountain to pray and continued all night in prayer to God. When it was day, He called for His disciples, and of them He chose twelve, whom He named apostles: Simon, whom He named Peter, and Andrew his brother, and James and John, and Philip and Bartholomew, and Matthew and Thomas, and James the son of Alphaeus, and Simon called the Zealot, and Judas the son of James, and Judas Iscariot, who became a traitor.[1]
—LUKE 6:12–16

How DO WE approach the Lord when we have a big decision to make? Do we pray for many hours? Do we fast? Do we seek counsel? With the challenge of this particular decision, choosing the twelve, the particular time selected by Christ to pray is meant to be a lesson to all of us. He had a decision to make that would resound throughout history. The decision coming the next day required perfect communication and unity with His Father. Can you see the great oneness of the Father, Son, and Holy Spirit in this decision? Can you grasp the depth of unity the Lord is asking us to enter with our fellow believers?

Jesus prayed the whole night. He set an example that we should follow. In great emergencies in our life, when we have duties with boundless consequence or we are about to face encounters with severe implications, we should seek divine blessing and direction by setting apart an unusual portion of time for prayer. Our Savior did it. We should follow in His footsteps.

People in the business world will sometimes spend hours upon hours in strategic planning, goal setting, and marketing plan development, even if it takes all-night sessions. Why should it seem strange that Christians spend an equal portion of time in the far more important business of prayer that has eternal significance? We need our minds renewed. We need to see the great necessity for prayer.

The Mystery

Jesus was completely a man, but He was also completely God. We can ask, "Why would Jesus pray?" As a man He had the same needs that we have—He needed divine support, strength, and blessing. The mystery here is that there was no more contradiction in His praying than there was in His drinking or eating. Both are consistent with who He was while here on this earth.

We pray for a lot of things. Mostly we pray for things we need (or think we need). We pray for the forgiveness of our sins. But Jesus had no sin. He was tempted, but He did not fall into temptation. There was no backsliding on His part. "Forgive us our debts, as we forgive our debtors" (Matt. 6:12) is an appropriate prayer for us, but He didn't need it for Himself. Paul describes this inner struggle that each of us face: "O wretched man that I am!" (Rom. 7:24). But Jesus didn't experience this. He had guarded His heart from sin and the enemy: "The ruler of this world is coming. He has no power over Me" (John 14:30). The enemy had no way to find entrance into Christ's heart.

The mystery: He was divine, yet He was tempted just like us. He was perfect, yet He was a man. He needed to pray all night on occasions, particularly on this occasion; His humanity compelled Him to pray. Jesus was fully human, mentally and emotionally. He sought the Father's wisdom, setting a profound example for us. If Jesus, who while fully human was also fully God, needed to pray for wisdom, how much more do we need to follow His example.

His Wisdom

Jesus frequently prayed before significant events. He called upon God the Father to be in complete communion with Him in choosing the Twelve. He called on the Father and the Holy Spirit for more understanding. He wanted to be in total unity with the Father and Holy Spirit in the choosing of the disciples. The example is clear for us if we have spiritual eyes to see: Christ wants us to grow in spiritual understanding and in the knowledge and application of His Word, but we must submit all that we are to His Spirit. We must commune with Him every day to know His will for our lives in all situations. It is in the secret place with God where we learn from Him. By the Lord's matchless grace given to us, we can live every day and make every decision in concert with His will for our lives. We can fellowship with Christ so intimately in the secret place that we can understand His will for our lives and be empowered by His Spirit to walk it out.

Prayer is mentioned over and over in the Psalms:

> O Lord, in the morning You will hear my voice; in the morning I will direct my prayer to You, and I will watch expectantly.
>
> —Psalm 5:3

Yet the LORD will command His lovingkindness in the daytime, and in the night His song will be with me, a prayer to the God of my life.

—PSALM 42:8

Hear my cry, O God, attend to my prayer.

—PSALM 61:1

But as for me, my prayer is to You, O LORD; in an acceptable time, O God, in the abundance of Your mercy, answer me in the truth of Your salvation.

—PSALM 69:13

Let my prayer be set forth before You as incense, and the lifting up of my hands as the evening sacrifice.

—PSALM 141:2

Jesus was no doubt familiar with these scriptures and the practices of the Jewish culture regarding prayer. He knew firsthand of the counsel and wisdom of the Father to be gained in prayer. He sought the Father and found the wisdom He needed. He received the Father's words through prayer. He knew when to heal through prayer. He chose the Twelve after a night of prayer. Jesus knew the key to wise decisions was to seek counsel from the One who has a good plan for each of us. So after praying all night, Jesus called His disciples together and then invited the Twelve, one by one, into a deeper place of intimacy with Him. Just as a good shepherd knows each of his sheep individually, Jesus knew each and every one of His disciples intimately. And He desires to know each of us in this same way.

Your invitation to be known is found in prayer. Your invitation to know His wisdom is found in prayer. Your invitation to know Him is found in prayer.

WHEN YOU PRAY

Just as Jesus showed by example, your decision-making model should be prayer.

When you have a decision to make, do you pray about it?

What can you do to be more aware of the need for prayer when making decisions?

_____

_____

_____

_____

_____

_____

_____

_____

_____

_____

_____

_____

THE BEGINNING AND END OF PRAYER

Therefore pray in this manner: Our Father who is in heaven, hal-
lowed be Your name. Your kingdom come; Your will be done
on earth, as it is in heaven. Give us this day our daily bread.
And forgive us our debts, as we forgive our debtors. And lead
us not into temptation, but deliver us from evil. For Yours is
the kingdom and the power and the glory forever. Amen.[1]
—MATTHEW 6:9–13

H E IS SIMPLY King of the universe. He is pure and holy. His ways and His thoughts are higher than ours (Isa. 55:8–9). The Lord our God is merciful, gracious, and abounding in goodness and truth (Exod. 34:6). Our finite minds are severely tested to grasp the vastness and power of our Father. Even though we may not be able to fully grasp all that our God is, we can still worship the Creator of the universe. We can worship the One who created light before there was a sun, whose spoken word divided the firmament into atmosphere and heavens, who created the dry land and vegetation, who made the sea creatures in all the depths, and who made man in His own likeness.

WORSHIP—THE BEGINNING OF PRAYER

Worship is the beginning of prayer. It is the first step, the starting point. Consider the fact that almost all man-made ideas for prayer or quiet times begin with worship, such as one of the more popular plans, ACTS: adoration, confession, thanksgiving, and supplication. Yet of far more importance is the fact that the King of the universe began His model prayer with worship: "Our Father who is heaven, hallowed be Your name."

The word for *worship* in the New Testament is *proskyneō*. It means "to kiss the hand to (towards) one, in token of reverence."[2] Worship is like blowing kisses to God. It is an act of love, and it is a response to love.

Stop right now and ask yourself this question: How do you view God? How you view God will determine how you approach Him in prayer. There are many people who do not view God the Father in a positive light. They may have had a dysfunctional relationship with their earthly fathers. For me, the revelation that God is my Father had life-changing impact. While I was growing up, my family had intimacy issues. My parents loved me deeply but struggled to express it. The result—I have had intimacy issues. But in recent years I have experienced a profound spiritual restoration and physical healing that leaves me convinced I have a good and kind heavenly Father. Maybe that seems a little elementary to you, but God's role as Father is the most profound aspect of His person to me. As my heavenly Father He is pure and holy, and I am convinced He is good. He is worthy of all my worship.

Understanding the Father's character is essential if we are to love and worship Him and enter into prayer with a pure heart. And that is what God is after. He is seeking true worshippers (John 4:23). Jesus taught us that we must begin with worship and adoration (Matt. 6:9). He taught us this because what comes natural for most of us is asking for "stuff." We don't have to train children to ask for things; it comes naturally.

Before we ever pray for anything, we need to meet the Lord in worship. For us to pray rightly, according to His will, we must come to a place in worship where we yield to the majesty and sovereignty of our Father. In the place of worship is where we find freedom from our selfishness. There is a monumental difference between approaching prayer with our own agenda in mind (no matter how righteous it may seem) and waiting on God to know what is on His mind. This is the prayer of discernment, of indifference to personal desires. It simply says, "Not my will, but Yours, be done" (Luke 22:42). Jesus demonstrated to the disciples that after they worshipped the Father, "hallowed be Your name," they would be able to proclaim, "Your kingdom come; Your will be done on earth, as it is in heaven" (Matt. 6:9–10).

WORSHIP—THE END OF PRAYER

We need to remind ourselves that what we call the Lord's Prayer isn't really the Lord's prayer—it is the disciples' prayer and our prayer. The disciples were the ones who wanted to be taught to pray. And just as Jesus taught them to begin their prayer with worship, He instructed them to end prayer with worship: "For Yours is the kingdom and the power and the glory forever" (Matt. 6:13).

Jesus taught the disciples and us that in prayer we are to pay homage to the reality that this is His kingdom. God has control over everything, and He can and will answer our prayers. He has infinite power to accomplish whatever we ask. There is nothing impossible with God (Luke 1:37).

All worship and praise are due our God for His mighty and wondrous works. As citizens of His kingdom we will worship Him forever. When, by the revelation of the Spirit of God, we understand that His kingdom, power, and glory are forever, what other response can we give but to worship Him? God Himself, His character, and all that He accomplishes on the earth are worthy of all glory. All that He is reverberates through eternity.

There seems little reason to believe that Jesus wanted His disciples to make His instruction in prayer some type of liturgical recitation (we have done this). He had just warned His followers in Matthew 6:7 to not use meaningless repetitions. Jesus had no use for prayer that was limited to a synagogue, ceremony, or rote. No, He wants each one of us, personally and intimately, to understand and appreciate the great mystery of His creation and His kingdom. Once we experience this revelation, there can be no other place to start or end prayer but with worship. Worship and prayer together become the gateway to His presence.

WHEN YOU PRAY

Prayer begins and ends with worship.

Ask the Lord, "What do You want to teach me about worship as part of my prayer life?"

Make a list of five things about the Lord that are worthy of worship. Use your list as a starting point for beginning and ending your prayer time in worship.

_____

_____

_____

Day 9

PRAY THIS WAY

Therefore pray in this manner: Our Father who is in heaven, hallowed be Your name. Your kingdom come; Your will be done on earth, as it is in heaven. Give us this day our daily bread. And forgive us our debts, as we forgive our debtors. And lead us not into temptation, but deliver us from evil. For Yours is the kingdom and the power and the glory forever. Amen.[1]
—MATTHEW 6:9–13

W E CANNOT FULLY understand the mastery of prayer that permeated Jesus's life. It is part of the great mystery of the Trinity. In the endless eons of time before the creation of the world, the Father, the Son, and the Holy Spirit were one, as they are now. The mind of God was the mind of Christ. However, when God became man in Christ, Christ's mode of communicating with the Father changed. He prayed now. Prayer was for Him, as it is for us, an intentional dialogue with God. His day began in prayer; His day ended in prayer. He prayed about all things. Jesus is the master Teacher when it comes to prayer.

The disciples asked the right person to teach them how to pray. But Jesus didn't just teach them the "how" of prayer—that prayer began and ended with worship. He also taught them what to pray for. As you read Jesus's list of what to pray for, ask the Holy Spirit for fresh revelation as to how you can practically respond to His instruction.

The Purposes of God

He desires His kingdom to come. It is His will, His purpose.

Our Father. It really is about community, the body of Christ, the church. One of the first things to understand about what Christ teaches us in this prayer is that we are part of a community of believers. He has set before us a vision of a renewed community and people in unity.

Our is a first-person plural pronoun. Jesus gave this model prayer in Matthew 6 (also found in Luke 11) for the disciples (plural) to pray. One of His disciples asked Him to teach them to pray. That disciple didn't say, "Teach me to pray." Throughout Matthew's account of the model prayer, three plural pronouns are used: *our*, *us*, and *we*. Jesus used these three personal pronouns nine times in His short prayer. The picture is clear: if you pray this prayer, you are in community with all of those who call God "Father."

Your kingdom come; Your will be done. Jesus's prayer reminds us that extending God's kingdom is included in our decision to follow Him. He has chosen us that we would go and bring forth fruit. We pray that we might lead others to know His saving power in their lives. The kingdom of heaven is at hand, and we must pray earnestly for the Spirit's empowerment to be His ambassadors. It seems so simple, so elementary, but it catches many of us off guard, "Your kingdom come; Your will be done." Help us, O Lord, to be willing ambassadors for your kingdom.

But we also pray for God's will to be done, for His purposes to be fulfilled. So much is contained in those four words: *Your will be done.* When we pray this way, we are asking for God's will in every area—our lives, our families, our ministries, our churches, our schools, our workplaces, our communities, our cities, our states, our nations, our world. God has a will and a purpose for everything, from the big things to the little things of our lives and our world.

PROVISION

Give us each day our daily bread. This is a prayer for provision. Because we live in such an affluent country, it is hard for us to conceptualize what a great struggle food for the day has been for most of the human beings who have lived on this planet. Even today there are hundreds of millions of people who do not have enough food on a regular basis. But how do those of us who are not facing starvation or hunger on a daily basis apply this? What do we pray for?

Do you remember those first-person plural pronouns? We are part of a community. We are part of the body of Christ. First Corinthians reminds us, "If one part suffers, all the parts suffer with it" (1 Cor. 12:26). The prayer for daily bread is not just for me or for you; it is for all of us. The Lord invites us to identify with the great needs of others when we pray. It is a petition that we struggle with at so many levels. How do we help when the need is so staggering? Through the power of prayer and the Holy Spirit, we understand that praying for the provision of those in need may be the most profound action we can take.

Now, let's go deeper and make this petition personal: give me my daily bread. Is that a prayer we can really live with? Can we live in this kind of simplicity and trust, like a little child? We have needs, and the Lord promises that we will be fed. His promises are true. "I have been young, and now am old; yet I have not seen the righteous forsaken, nor their off-spring begging bread" (Ps. 37:25).

Proverbs says, "Keep falsehood and lies far from me; give

me neither poverty nor riches, but give me only my daily bread" (Prov. 30:8, NIV). Can we be grateful for the food set before us today? A little child does not worry where his food is coming from next week. He has great trust in a loving father. How much more should we trust our heavenly Father.

There is one place we repeatedly allow our peace and contentment to be stolen. We compare our provision to others. I think of it as the original sin—comparison. Eve saw the fruit of the tree, and it was more pleasing than what she had. The two most important steps in finding contentment in life are not comparing what you have to others and having a grateful heart. God will provide (Gen. 22:14). The challenge set before us is to pray and be grateful for God's provision.

PARDON

Forgive us our debts, as we forgive our debtors. To be forgiven, you must forgive. You must live in forgiveness daily toward everyone: your spouse, friends, enemies, children, and most of all yourself. There is great freedom in forgiveness; it is the key to the kingdom—confessing our sins, seeking forgiveness, and forgiving others. Unforgiveness holds us prisoner; it makes us a prisoner to the past. It takes sin, offenses, and hurts from the past, brings them into my present, and damages my future. Unforgiveness is a poison. When you forgive others who have wronged you, the person you help the most is yourself.

We can face some horrific situations in life that would seem to give us the freedom to be offended, hurt, and unforgiving. However, when you consider the cost of unforgiveness—God not forgiving your sins and living in bondage to the past—the cost of unforgiveness is just too great. "But if you do not forgive men for their sins, neither will your Father forgive your sins" (Matt. 6:15). Unforgiveness in most people eventually leads to bitterness. Unforgiveness and bitterness makes us spiritually dirty: "Pursue peace with all men, and the holiness without which no one will see the Lord, watching diligently so that no one falls short of the grace of God, lest any root of bitterness spring up to cause trouble, and many become defiled by it" (Heb. 12:14–15). As we forgive others, we position ourselves to be washed clean by the blood and sacrifice of Christ.

Christ knows well the power of forgiveness. He instructed the disciples pointedly to seek forgiveness and give forgiveness. The Holy Spirit is our helper when it comes to prayer. If we will but pray this simple prayer of forgiveness every day, we will discover a new level of intimacy with Christ: "Forgive us our debts, as we forgive our debtors."

PROTECTION

Christ instructs us to pray a very honest prayer, "Lead us not into temptation." As shocking as the thought may be, the Lord tests us and allows very difficult tests to come our way (Ps. 139:23–24; Jer. 17:10; 1 Pet. 1:6–9). The Lord desires to produce pure gold out of our lives, and the times of testing can be deep and severe. Far too many of us are not in a position to face temptation when it comes. Our response to the temptation was made already by past decisions. The disciples presented Jesus a very sincere request, "Teach us to pray." Jesus gave a very honest answer they needed to hear and pray. They should follow Christ's instruction and pray to be saved from temptations.

For our protection the Lord is able to chain up the roaring lion that seeks to tempt and destroy us. The enemy is subtle; he is scheming. But the Lord knows how to save us from the tempting wiles of the enemy: "The Lord knows how to rescue the godly from trial" (2 Pet. 2:9). There is great strength and hope in the Lord's keeping power: "Keep your servant from willful sins; may they not rule over me. Then I will be blameless, innocent of great transgression" (Ps. 19:13, NIV). We need to pray for the Lord's protection on a daily basis as we face our day-to-day struggles.

Do you count yourself among those who need Christ to teach them to pray? I do. I am so grateful for the simplicity of His instruction on prayer. Honestly I am a very plain man, and I can understand Christ's instruction on how to pray that He gave the disciples. So let us come together and learn from the master Teacher on prayer. Let's pray for God's purposes, provision, pardon, and protection.

When You Pray

Simply follow Christ's directions on prayer.

As you pray, ask the Lord to fulfill His purposes for you and your particular community of believers.

Pray today for someone you know who is struggling for provision.

Pray today the simple prayer of pardon: forgive me my debts as I forgive my debtors.

Cry out to the Lord today to be protected from temptation.

_____

_____

_____

WHAT YOU REALLY NEED

When He had taken the five loaves and the two fish, He looked up to heaven, and blessed and broke the loaves, and gave them to His disciples to set before them. And He divided the two fish among them all.[1]
—MARK 6:41

CHRIST SAW THAT the people were like sheep without a shepherd, and He felt compassion for them. He had experienced the large crowds wildly running after Him from every city. It is probable that this particular crowd was just like the disciples that day—there was so much activity and excitement they didn't even take time to eat. You know there is a lot going on when you don't even have time to eat.

Christ was in the process of trying to set aside some time for the disciples to "debrief" with Him. The disciples had just returned from having been sent out by Jesus for the first time. So they got in a boat and went to a secluded place. But they couldn't evade the people. The people from all the cities ran ahead of them and waited on the shore:

Then He said to them, "Come away by yourselves to a remote place and rest a while," for many were coming and going, and they had no leisure even to eat. So they went into a remote place privately by boat. But the people saw them departing, and many knew Him and ran there on foot out of every city. They arrived first and came together to Him.

—MARK 6:31–33

When they landed, Jesus saw the people and had compassion on the crowd. But how did He show it? He showed it in a way we wouldn't normally think of. We think in physical, temporal realms. He thinks in spiritual and eternal dimensions.

THE DILEMMA OF OUR NEEDS AND WANTS

Because of Jesus's compassion He knew what the crowd really needed. His relationship with the Father was built on purposeful prayer in the secret place and constant prayer during the day. Through communion with the Father He had a true understanding of the people's need, so He first fed the crowd spiritual food: "When Jesus came out and saw many people, He was moved with compassion on them, because they were like sheep without a shepherd. And He began to teach them many things" (Mark 6:34). Jesus knew the crowd was following Him because only He had the words of eternal life.

What do you really need?

Some years back I made a trip to India to visit one of my sons, who worked in Bangalore. He had a close group of young friends that I met and spent time with. In India if you are poor, you walk everywhere you go. With a little bit of money you graduate to owning a bicycle. The next step up the transportation ladder of success is to own a motorcycle. Tourists and wealthy people use the auto rickshaws or even rent a car. Ownership of a car is reserved for the wealthy.

One day I was visiting a friend of my son who was considered upper middle class. He had a small business that rented a tiny one-room office. He employed two other young men, and like every other business he also had a *chaiwala*, a young boy who delivered tea for the office. One afternoon we went to the friend's apartment. It was a small but nice apartment.

While we were sitting on the couch, he started querying me about life in America. When the subject of cars came up, he wanted to know if I had a car. At the time I had two older vehicles, a small, eight-year-old car with more than 110,000 miles and a nine-year-old minivan with 125,000 miles. When I told him about my two cars, he responded, "You must be a very wealthy man, Mr. Cameron."

Obviously the gulf between our needs and wants encompasses much more than transportation. We can treat this gulf between our needs and wants as a litmus test for our love for the world or our love for the Lord. Which do we love more, the things of the world or the things of the Lord?

> Do not love the world or the things in the world. If anyone loves the world, the love of the Father is not in him. For all that is in the world—the lust of the flesh, the lust of the eyes, and the pride of life—is not of the Father, but is of the world. The world and its desires are passing away, but the one who does the will of God lives forever.
>
> —1 John 2:15–17

If we are walking intimately with Christ, we have a different perspective on the world—the lust of the flesh, the lust of the eyes, and the pride of life—than others do. The mind of Christ and the discernment He gives provide us clarity concerning the difference between our needs and wants. With His spirit in us we are able to discern whether something is expedient or really necessary.

Jesus knew what the people needed first. It was for this that He came: to preach the kingdom of God, to heal the infirm, and to bring life to many: "The Spirit of the Lord is upon Me, because He has anointed Me to preach the gospel to the poor; He has sent Me to heal the broken-hearted, to preach deliverance to the captives and recovery of sight to the blind, to set at liberty those who are oppressed" (Luke 4:18). He gave them what they needed first, His Word. One of the most basic understandings of following Christ is that we need His Word and prayer first on a daily basis.

DAILY FOOD

The connection between God's Word and our spirits is exactly the same as the connection that exists between food and our bodies. We know that we must have physical food to function, and we function best when we eat daily. It doesn't make any difference what shape you are in; if you don't take in food, you will eventually grow weak. Even the healthiest athlete at the pinnacle of physical fitness and performance fails quickly without food. The Christian with the most responsibilities at church and who is the most educated concerning the Bible and apt to teach will eventually wither up and die spiritually without a regular intake of the Word and prayer.

But a healthy spiritual life is more than picking up the Word to read and praying each day. Contrast my eating habits with Isaac, the son of my daughter and son-in-law, both of whom are physicians. My mom was a short-order cook for three siblings, and my eating habits are atrocious. I was well into my forties before I ate my first salad. Growing up, my vegetables of choice consisted of corn, potatoes, and green beans. And I am a recovering carnivore; most of my life I ate some kind of meat at almost every meal, chased down by a soft drink. Then there is our four-year-old grandson Isaac. He drinks water. Ask him what he wants for a snack, and he might say hummus and carrots. It's unbelievable. He eats every kind of vegetable, and based on all outward appearances, he likes them. Imagine that from a four-year-old! His eating habits are characterized by making healthy choices on a daily basis.

Jesus is the bread of life. He is our spiritual food. "Jesus said to them, 'I am the bread of life. Whoever comes to Me shall never hunger, and whoever believes in Me shall never thirst'" (John 6:35). What is the quality of your spiritual diet with the Lord in the secret place? Are you consuming the Word?

There is more. It is not just about the right kind of food. You have to factor in the freshness of the food. There is something special about fresh food eaten daily. It tastes different. It has more nutritional value. We do everything we can do to keep food fresh and make it last: we can it, freeze it, dry it, or freeze-dry it; we put substances in it to preserve the flavor and enhance its taste and appearance (additives). However, there is nothing like fresh food. We need to treat the Word the same way we treat food: fresher is better. At times we do everything we can to hear the Word without digging deeply into it ourselves in quietness before the Lord with prayer. We try devotionals, prerecorded teaching, video recordings, television and radio programs, daily e-mail devotions, and on and on. Granted, these other practices we try are good, but they will never fully substitute for daily, personal meditation on the Word with prayer and meeting the Lord in the secret place.

The pickings were slim as I rummaged for food at the condo where we were staying. However, there's always my old standby, peanut butter and jelly; for my wife it is a mayonnaise and tomato sandwich. While making a sandwich, I happened to look at the mayonnaise expiration date. It was one year and two months expired. Oops. It looked and smelled OK, but I didn't let my wife risk it. Off it went to the trash.

I firmly believe that most spiritual encounters have an

expiration date on them like the food we buy at the store. A single encounter with the Lord will not sustain us for months and months. The Lord wants us to meet with Him every day. Your body cannot be sustained for long by yesterday's food. Correspondingly your spirit cannot be sustained for long by yesterday's spiritual food. When God supplied the children of Israel with manna in the desert, He gave them just enough for each day. He wanted them and us to know that we need His spiritual food, fresh every day. We need to follow the example of the psalmist: "Lord, I call daily upon you" (Ps. 88:9). Let us be known as those who "received the word with all eagerness, daily examining the Scriptures" (Acts 17:11).

When You Pray

You need a fresh supply of the Word and prayer every day.

What comes easier for you, studying the Word or praying? Why do you think that is so?

Think of a few things you could do to incorporate a full measure of the Word and prayer into your quiet time with the Lord.

Read a chapter of Proverbs during your prayer time every day for a month. (There are thirty-one chapters, so just read the chapter that corresponds with the date).

_____

_____

_____

_____

HE IS ALWAYS ENOUGH

When He had taken the five loaves and the two fish, He looked up to heaven, and blessed and broke the loaves, and gave them to His disciples to set before them. And He divided the two fish among them all.[1]
—MARK 6:41

THINKING ABOUT EATING food isn't going to do much for your body. You have to eat food to live. You can know how to make food. You can know everything there is about its nutritional value. You can even have a month's supply of the healthy food stored in the pantry. But your knowledge of food and a storehouse of food will not help you if you don't eat. The same goes for our spiritual food. You can have a Bible in every room of your house. You can have a master of divinity degree and be skilled at teaching or preaching the Word. You can possess the best software programs for studying the Bible in the original language with wonderful historical commentaries. You can have e-mail devotionals delivered to your smartphone every morning. However, all of this education, skill, and resources will not necessarily help you spiritually unless you daily take His Word and prayer deep inside your spirit.

EAT UP

Jesus was tempted by the devil to turn a stone into bread while He was fasting in the wilderness. He quoted Scripture to the devil: "It is written, 'Man shall not live by bread alone, but by every word that proceeds out of the mouth of God'" (Matt. 4:4). Jesus taught us that we must take His Word deep inside us daily. We are more than just physical beings who need food to survive. We are spiritual creations who need to commune with our God every day. Most of us are too busy to eat properly. Busyness also keeps us from praying. Busyness keeps us from taking time to study, meditate, and hide God's Word in our hearts. We have an epidemic in the church of spiritually malnourished people who don't meet Jesus in the secret place daily in the Word and prayer. The admonitions in the Scripture are numerous and pointed. Meditate on the Word and pray. Your spiritual life depends on it. Here are just a few of the promised results on meditating and hiding God's Word in your heart:

+ You can have peace in your life: "Those who love Your law have great peace, and nothing shall cause them to stumble" (Ps. 119:165).

+ You can be free from pornography and other sexual sins: "How shall a young man keep his way pure? By keeping it according to Your word. With my whole heart I seek You; do not allow me to wander from Your commandments. Your word I have hidden in my heart, that I might not sin against You" (Ps. 119:9–11).

+ Your prayers will be answered: "If you remain in Me, and My words remain in you, you will ask whatever you desire, and it shall be done for you" (John 15:7).

+ You will be wise and successful: "This Book of the Law must not depart from your mouth. Meditate on it day and night so that you may act carefully according to all that is written in it. For then you will make your way successful, and you will be wise" (Josh. 1:8).

+ You will have a life full of joy and contentment: "His
  delight is in the law of the LORD, and in His law
  he meditates day and night. He will be like a tree
  planted by the rivers of water, that brings forth
  its fruit in its season; its leaf will not wither, and
  whatever he does will prosper" (Ps. 1:2–3).

You need to consistently meet the Lord in the secret place
with prayer and the Word. You need to hunger after His
Word—hunger and thirst for it profoundly and passion-
ately. We need a fresh revelation of Jesus in our lives every
day, even more than we need food, water, and air. Jesus is the
only One who can provide the kind of spiritual nourishment
our souls long for. He said, "I am the bread of life. Whoever
comes to Me shall never hunger, and whoever believes in Me
shall never thirst" (John 6:35). Our hunger and thirst are satisfied in His presence in the secret place.

The Lord's Word is inseparably linked to prayer. It is in
prayer that we seek to have a relationship with God and to
know Him intimately. It is in the Word that He most often
speaks to us. A full measure of daily prayer with little of the
Word gives life; however, it leads to a lack of steadfastness.
Much of the Word with little prayer leaves us unhealthy and
prone to judgment and legalism. Being able to stand the tests
and storms of life necessitates having the Word embedded
deep in our souls with a full measure of prayer daily. A full
measure of the Word and prayer daily is indispensable in
living the Spirit-filled life.

Are you desperate? Do you see that you are spiritually
bankrupt and Jesus is the only answer? I don't think we really
get it. There is a supply of God's spirit and presence that will
both kill us and fill us. It will kill us and put to death the

flesh with its appetites, passions, and addictions. And in the process the Holy Spirit will help us to empty ourselves of our own spirit as much as is possible. It will be painful, but it is a hurt that satisfies and electrifies our souls. Then we will be filled up to overflowing with His Spirit and presence. We will be so spiritually healthy that we will have something to offer every person who crosses our paths.

Here's the Deal

Because it was getting late, the disciples encouraged Jesus to send the people away. The Bible tells us there were five thousand men there, so the total number of people, including the children and women, was likely between fifteen thousand and twenty thousand. The disciples wanted Him to send the crowd into the surrounding countryside and villages to get themselves something to eat. But Jesus told the disciples, "You give them something to eat." They responded, "That would take more than half a year's wages! Are we to go and spend that much on bread and give it to them to eat?" (Mark 6:37, NIV). The disciples were startled and didn't know what to do. Jesus took the five loaves and two fish, gave thanks, and multiplied them to feed the thousands and thousands of people with more than twelve basketsful left over.

Jesus showed the disciples that He is sufficient for all things. He is enough. His Word is sufficient. His supply is inexhaustible. He was always teaching His followers. Did they have eyes to see and ears to hear? This is what we discover in the secret place with the Word and prayer—*He is always enough.*

WHEN YOU PRAY

We find His sufficiency for every need every day in prayer and the Word.

What is the greatest lack in your prayer life? Come to the Lord today in prayer and cry out for His grace to overcome this lack.

Choose a verse to meditate on and hide in your heart. Start memorizing it today.

_____

_____

_____

_____

_____

_____

_____

_____

_____

_____

_____

NEVER ALONE

*When He sent the crowds away, He went up into a mountain by
Himself to pray. And when evening came, He was there alone.*[1]
—MATTHEW 14:23

JESUS OFTEN WENT away to be alone and pray. Solitude was
the touchstone of His prayer life. This one event of Christ's
prayer life captures two of the most pointed lessons we have
to learn about prayer: we need to be alone at times, and we
must persist in prayer.

ALONE WITH GOD

It is so much easier to pray with others than to pray alone.
When you are praying alone, there is no one to impress, no
reason to draw attention to yourself, no purpose in attempting
to show off how much you know. Please don't misunderstand
me. Praying with others is powerful and needed, and we do
not do it enough. But when you pray alone, you are never
really alone. Never forget that the Lord is always with you.

Silence is a stranger to most of us. To discover silence, we
have to be like Jesus and go off to find a place where we can
turn off the cell phone and the TV, a place with no bustling
businesses or chattering people to deal with. The Lord calls us
to this silence as much as He calls us to be with one another.

What should our times of silence and being alone before
the Lord consist of? This is where the prayer life of Jesus is
such a profound example for us. Jesus shows us that these

times of intimacy must first center on being quiet and listening. We cannot put God in a box and make our relationship with Him a formula. But if we are going to follow the example of Jesus, we must get alone with God and silence ourselves. The silence that He invites us into is a silence of listening, a respectful stillness before our God, a place where the Holy Spirit makes His words alive to our souls. This kind of silence brings great joy, clarity, and purity to our life. This silence will bring us to the place of understanding the principle issues of our life.

Thank God we can have this sweet fellowship with the Lord. Being quiet and still before God will produce a "hearing ear," one that listens to the Spirit. This is correct hearing that leads to speaking accurately and at the right time. It is also the kind of hearing that leads to leaving many words unspoken. It is this tender fellowship with God that prepares us to open the Word, meditate on it, and be guided by the Holy Spirit in prayer.

I believe many Christians fear time alone with God because they have not been taught how to pray. They have tried praying on their own, but they quickly run out of words and don't know what to do. No one has ever taught them that prayer is not a soliloquy (a one-sided conversation); rather, it is an exchange between a kind and loving God and us. Prayer is the place where we listen to what our Father has to say to us. And we are never alone.

PERSEVERING IN PRAYER

Time and time again in Christ's ministry He taught that we must persist in prayer. He modeled this perseverance in prayer by often stealing away to a quiet place to pray. In one of the simplest and yet insightful parables, the parable of the persistent widow and the judge, Jesus taught us that we should pray and not give up (Luke 18:1–8). We must come again and again and again, and press the issue for our answers in prayer. We must pray with intensity, passion, reiteration, and urgency.

Perseverance is one of the conditions for answered prayer, and at the same time it is one of the greatest mysteries of prayer. Without it many prayers will never be answered. Persevering in prayer is also one of the clearest paths to spiritual growth. Our God is a consuming fire (Deut. 4:24), and persevering in unanswered prayer will turn the heat up in our lives quickly. The dross of our life will come to the surface and easily be seen. This is a great place to have our character refined so we come out as pure gold (Job 23:10; Rev. 3:18).

Persevering in unanswered prayer does another marvelous work in our life—it exercises our faith and takes us up to a higher place with God. Five years of chronic pain left me with repeated daily pain crises and suicidal thoughts. It also purified my life, dredging my soul. My once proud spiritual presentation was purified to only having a small grain of faith left. God gave me that faith to exercise and use in the power of the Holy Spirit. When I finally put that small grain of faith into action under the unction of the Holy Spirit, I was launched onto the road of healing and restoration.

YOU ARE NEVER ALONE

As I navigated the years of chronic pain that had me weeping during the day, losing my job, and hiding in the bed with the covers over my head, my wife was by my side constantly. I had a couple of dear, lifelong friends who stood with me and caught the brunt of my desperate phone calls when my pain was out of control. I remember the phrase I uttered repeatedly to my wife and friends (and I have since learned that most people in my situation voice constantly): "You just don't understand!" That phrase is another way for saying, "I am in this alone."

The crucible of perseverance in unanswered prayer is the breeding ground for feelings of abandonment and being left alone. The enemy's lies seem so believable in this place. While it is true that few people may understand you in this state and others may avoid you because it is uncomfortable for them, the truth is that you are not alone. God promises to never leave or forsake us. You are never alone.

> Be strong and of a good courage. Fear not, nor be afraid of them, for the LORD your God, it is He who goes with you. He will not fail you, nor forsake you.
> —DEUTERONOMY 31:6

> For He has said: "I will never leave you, nor forsake you."
> —HEBREWS 13:5

Our Lord wants to meet with you. Noting could be more important. He's waiting on you. He is waiting on you in the secret place, the place where the Father teaches us to pray and the place where He is always found. Make it your quest today. Make it your priority. Persevere. You are never alone.

WHEN YOU PRAY

Nothing in your life is more important than coming to Jesus in prayer.

What is often the first thing on your mind when you wake in the morning?

What step could you take to focus your thoughts on the Lord when you wake?

_____

_____

_____

_____

_____

_____

_____

_____

_____

_____

_____

_____

_____

_____

_____

_____

_____

BE STILL

*He commanded the people to sit down on the ground. Taking
the seven loaves and giving thanks, He broke them and gave
them to His disciples to serve. And they served the crowd.*[1]
—MARK 8:6

HE TOLD THE crowd to sit down. A very simple command and act. Can you sit down to listen and pray?
The Lord revealed to us His purpose for answering prayer:
He wants the Father to be glorified in the Son. Jesus wants
our prayers to be answered as we pray in His name. The mystifying truth is that the possibilities in prayer are as great as
the purpose for prayer. But we must avail ourselves of the
Lord in the secret place. We must learn to be still.

FINDING STILLNESS

Finding stillness may be one of the greatest challenges in our
relationships with Christ and our prayer lives. There are two
great hindrances we face every day in our search for stillness: our busy lifestyles and the constant noise of our culture.
From the incessant barrage of information to the insidious
advertising, our toxic culture leaves us no rest. Are you busy?
Where are you on the Facebook addiction scale? Enough said.

I was raised in front of a television. I did my homework
there and spent much of my free time late in the evenings
sitting with my family watching television. My learning style
is to have background noise. Silence is very difficult for me,

even today. As with me, most of us have become accustomed to the never-ending noise, and even if we are not used to it, we find it difficult to escape. So how do we find stillness?

As simple as it may seem, we find stillness by making a choice, deciding to sit down away from all the clamor of our life and technology. God bestowed on us free will; it is not an illusion. We are not victims of our culture. We have control over the way we respond to everything that comes our way. The science of neuroplasticity (the ability of the brain to reorganize itself by developing new neural connections) makes it very clear that when we make a decision, we change the matter in our brain.[2] It is the scientific confirmation of God's Word: "For as he thinks in his heart, so is he" (Prov. 23:7). Every time we steal away with the Lord in quiet retreat, we transform and renew our minds and conform to the communication pathways of the kingdom (Rom. 12:1–2). And it is in the stillness that our zeal for the Lord and His ways is given the chance to grow.

HOW FAR WOULD YOU GO?

What would you do? Stories of this Jesus were spreading like wildfire. Thousands were seeking Him. Mark comments, "[People] were astonished beyond measure, saying, 'He has done all things well. He makes both the deaf to hear and the mute to speak'" (Mark 7:37). What did the crowd do? They followed Him for three days without food! Jesus said, "I have compassion on the crowd, because they have now been with Me three days and have nothing to eat" (Mark 8:2).

Some years ago my wife and I heard about an unusual outpouring of the Spirit of the Lord hundreds of miles from where we lived. We heard stories of great healings, masses being saved, and miraculous visitations of the Lord. So we loaded up two of our daughters and drove sixteen hours to that city to spend a week. It was the only time in my life I've seen non-churched people come to Christ, and we saw hundreds come to know Him as their Savior. As the altar was opened for salvation or prayer each evening, you had to run to the front or you would be left watching. We would start standing in line early in the morning and would be there all day to get into a service that evening. Imagine that. The revival had a service each week in which they would just listen to testimonies from those in attendance.

One man's testimony was that he had just been released from prison. He appeared to be middle aged, maybe in his early fifties. He said he had been in prison most of his life. My first thought was, "What did this guy do to spend decades in prison? Did he kill someone?" The man didn't know why, but when he got out of prison, there was an impression in his mind that he should go to a particular city. He decided to hitchhike there. Upon arriving, something just didn't seem right, so he went to a library, looked at a map, and discovered that there was another major city with the same name, but it was halfway across the country. He had a little money left, so he hopped a bus to that city with the same name. Once he arrived, he got into a taxi. He asked the driver, "Where does a guy go for a good time?" The driver thought he would play a joke on him and dropped him off at the church where the revival was. There were so many people in line and so much commotion that he decided to get in line and see what the buzz was.

He was saved miraculously that night. When he gave his testimony at the church a few nights later, he related how he had come to the service and the Lord had delivered him of a spirit of murder. He was free for the first time he could remember. He was rejoicing as a new creation in Christ. As he wept, weeping began to break out across the throng of people in the auditorium. Within minutes hundreds upon hundreds were weeping.

We have a difficult time believing that the same power of God that raised Jesus from the dead and empowered the disciples is available to us today. But it is. It is. And when people encounter the Holy Spirit and His power, radical change and results take place.

It is not surprising that people dropped everything and followed Jesus. The majority of them had been raised hearing and reading of God's miracles accomplished for their ancestors, but that was in the past—this was now. They had heard rabbis speak in the temple, but they had never heard anyone speak with this kind of authority. They had never seen miracles performed with their own eyes.

What would you do? Would you take off work? Would you travel hundreds of miles to hear Him? Would you tell everyone who would listen about Him? Would you go without food for days to follow Him? What is your hunger level for the Lord?

ZEALOUS FOR THE LORD

Take a look at these zealous men in the Bible:

+ Phinehas was personally commended by God for his pursuit of God's righteousness. The Lord told Moses, "I hereby grant [Phinehas] My covenant of peace. And it will be for him and his seed after him, even the covenant of an everlasting priesthood, because he was zealous for his God and made an atonement for the children of Israel" (Num. 25:12–13).

+ Caleb served the Lord with his whole heart when the hearts of those around him melted with fear: "Moses the servant of the LORD sent me from Kadesh Barnea to spy on the land, and I brought word back to him as it was in my heart. My companions who went up with me made the hearts of the people melt, but I wholeheartedly followed after the LORD my God" (Josh. 14:7–8).

+ Jonathan showed his zeal for the Lord by challenging a Philistine garrison with only his armor bearer (1 Sam. 14:1–15).

+ Apollos was fervent in spirit and spoke boldly in the synagogues, convincing the Jews about Christ. "This man was instructed in the way of the Lord, knowing only the baptism of John, but being fervent in spirit, he accurately spoke and taught the things concerning the Lord. He began to speak boldly in the synagogue…he greatly helped those who had believed through grace. For he vehemently refuted the Jews publicly, proving from the Scriptures that Jesus was the Christ" (Acts 18:25–28).

Paul instructed the believers in Romans to be fervent for the Lord (Rom. 12:11). The word *fervent* in the literal and etymological sense means "very hot or boiling."[3] Paul is comparing the Christian's temperament to boiling water. Paul's instruction and expectation are that Christians would be like him, boiling hot for the Lord: "Cleave to what is good. Be devoted to one another with brotherly love; prefer one another in honor, do not be lazy in diligence, be fervent in spirit, serve the Lord, rejoice in hope, be patient in suffering, persevere in prayer" (Rom. 12:9–12). I find it fascinating that when giving an example of fervent, a secular dictionary uses "fervent prayers."[4]

The Lord delights in passion for prayer and passion for Him and His kingdom. The truth is He can't stand lukewarm or dispassionate people. Being lukewarm is a fatal spiritual state for a person. A lukewarm Christian is deceived and lives a life of duplicity.

+ "Nevertheless I have this against you, that you have left your first love" (Rev. 2:4, NKJV). The sin that Christ held against this church was their loss of zeal and love.

+ "I know your works, that you are neither cold nor hot. I could wish you were cold or hot. So then, because you are lukewarm, and neither cold nor hot, I will vomit you out of My mouth" (Rev. 3:15–16, NKJV).

Jesus is the bread of life, and His promises are true. There is a spiritual need, a hunger, in our lives that can only be satisfied by communing with our Lord and Savior in the secret place. So where can we find this kind of passion for prayer, a zeal that will not be satisfied with any counterfeit or substitute? It all originates in the secret place, in our stillness before the Lord. Jesus gives the invitation and instruction to come and sit down with Him, to be still: "Be still and know that I am God" (Ps. 46:10).

WHEN YOU PRAY

Zeal and passion are born in stillness before the Lord.

How would you rate your passion for the Lord on a scale of one to ten with one being burnt out and ten being white hot?

What is a practical step you can take to increase your zeal for the Lord in prayer?

_____

_____

_____

_____

_____

_____

_____

_____

_____

_____

_____

_____

DAY 14

LESSON LEARNED

He commanded the people to sit down on the ground. Taking the seven loaves and giving thanks, He broke them and gave them to His disciples to serve. And they served the crowd.[1]
—MARK 8:6

JESUS TOOK THE seven loaves and gave thanks. He used this paltry supply along with a few fish to feed four thousand men and probably an additional four to eight thousand women and children. How could He give thanks for this insufficient supply of food? He had complete trust in the Father. Jesus knew that the Father made all things good. In the face of adversity, disappointment, or overwhelming odds, the Father can still be trusted. It was all under control.

How do you respond when situations do not go as you planned? Are you disappointed in others, yourself, or perhaps even God? Next to sin, disappointment may be the most serious problem we face as Christians. Why? Because if we don't discover God's purposes in disappointment, it can eventually lead to withdrawing from fellowship with other Christians or even God. What is the Lord's purpose in our lives through all of the disappointment we face? His purpose is to reproduce His character in us, for us to empty ourselves of our spirits and fully take in His Spirit.

The dictionary definition of *affliction* is "the cause of persistent pain or distress; great suffering."[2] Affliction puts pressure on us, and pressure is part of God's plan to make us more like Him. Afflictions, hardships, loss, illness, accidents, and other trials put great pressure on us. We can choose to respond with disappointment, or we can choose to turn to Jesus, remembering that "we also glory in tribulations, knowing that tribulation produces perseverance; and perseverance, character; and character, hope. Now hope does not disappoint, because the love of God has been poured out in our hearts by the Holy Spirit who was given to us" (Rom. 5:3–5, NKJV).

The Lord gave thanks in all things. He gave thanks when there was not enough. How could seven loaves be enough to feed thousands? He knew the character and spirit of God—His Father was always at work. That is our destination—to come to a place where we can give thanks in everything because we trust our Lord. Whether it is illness, hardship, or distress, we know our Lord will weave it into His purposes for our lives. For "we know that all things work together for good to those who love God, to those who are called according to His purpose" (Rom. 8:28). Amen!

THEY JUST DIDN'T GET IT!

Round two: A large crowd is following Jesus. They have had nothing to eat, and Jesus turns to the disciples to share His compassion for the crowd with the disciples. The disciples respond, "Where can one get bread to feed these men here in the wilderness?" (Mark 8:4).

What a revelatory statement from the disciples. Mark even commented specifically that the disciples didn't understand the miracle of the feeding of the five thousand: "For they had not comprehended the miracle of the loaves, for their hearts were hardened" (Mark 6:52). The disciples were slow to perceive Jesus's power and who He was. It makes you wonder at what point the disciples will understand who He is and what He is capable of doing. Jesus heals the blind, causes the deaf to hear, and makes the lame walk! Just days before He had miraculously fed upward of fifteen thousand people. And the disciples now say, "How can one satisfy these people with bread?" (Mark 8:4, NKJV).

This story raises a simple, profound question: Are you teachable? Personally, I am somewhat hardheaded. In my hardheadedness it is difficult for me to receive God's words immediately. What about you? How many times does He speak to your heart about the same issue before you get it? Five times? Ten times? Never? How long does it take you to respond to Him when He puts a finger on an issue in your life? Throughout my years as a manager I have been stunned by the hardheadedness of some people who have to be corrected about the same issue over and over *ad nauseam*. But then I look at my own life and realize I should not be surprised. Remaining teachable should be a great matter of prayer for each one of us. *Lord, let me be tender and pliable in Your hands.* One of the questions I repeatedly ask myself is: Am I still trainable and teachable? Jesus will speak to us as we open His Word and seek Him in prayer. He is faithful to suffer long with us.

Shortly after my wife and I were married, I had a prophetic brother put his hands on my head and prophesy, "Thus saith the Lord, listen to your wife." I heard those words, but honestly it took more than thirty years for me to begin to live them out. The truth is it happens time and time again—my wife's prudence, common sense, and godly wisdom help me navigate relationships and life's decisions. We are becoming more and more the team the Lord meant us to be. The heartache caused in our marriage due to my hard-heartedness is humbling and sobering. My pride kept me from listening to my wife.

What keeps us from being teachable? I believe our hearts have become hardened by sin, and in pride we set ourselves up as the final authority. Pride insulates us from hearing the truth. Pride makes us callous as we repeatedly choose our own way. We become unteachable.

CLASS IS IN SESSION

Jesus is always at hand to teach and correct us. He wants us to be teachable and hungry for His presence in prayer. Each one of us has to make a purposeful decision to be a diligent student of prayer and learn from Him. As I meet with others and share about Christ, I always ask, "Do you have a place where you write down answers to prayer, goals, lessons the Lord has taught you, and dreams?" Rarely do I hear that someone chronicles any of these events. Most people can testify to the Lord's miraculous provision and touch in their lives. Most will testify that they have had answers to prayers and that Christ has spoken to them in dreams, through the Word, and in dramatic events. Yet very few write these glorious happenings down, and they are lost—lost forever. There is something about recording answers to prayer and revisiting those from time to time that fortifies our faith. I have a little section in a personal notebook entitled "Great Answers to Prayer." When I revisit these answers to my prayers, I am again convinced that Christ answers prayer. I implore you: chronicle your prayers, write them down, revisit them, and meditate on the Lord's goodness to you.

Jesus desires to teach us about prayer. But first we must be trainable. We must be able to sit still and listen to Him. And we must fight letting the ups and downs of life interfere with an attitude of being teachable. Sit down today with a pen, your favorite journal, and the Bible, and He will speak to you. Write down the profound lessons on prayer taught to you by the Jesus through the Holy Spirit. Reflect on them regularly, and you will begin to understand the mysteries of prayer and take them deep into your soul.

WHEN YOU PRAY

Chronicle the lessons Jesus's prayers teach you, and learn the lesson the first time.

Do you have a life notebook or a journal—a place where you write down the lessons you learn about prayer, great answers to prayer, the people you are interceding for, scriptures that speak to your heart, and other topics so vital to your life in the Lord?

What do you need to do to establish a habit of recording what God shows you for the rest of the days you walk with the Lord?

What did the Lord speak to your heart today?

_____

_____

_____

_____

_____

_____

DAY 15

WHO IS THIS JESUS?

As He was alone praying, His disciples were with Him. And
He asked them, "Who do the people say that I am?" They
answered, "John the Baptist. But some say Elijah. And others say
that one of the old prophets has risen." He said to them, "But who
do you say that I am?" Peter answered, "The Christ of God."
—LUKE 9:18–20

IT WAS THE familiar scenario with Jesus—He had gone off alone to pray. In His time of communion with the Father, Jesus understands it is time to ask His disciples the question: "Who do you say I am?" This question will provoke the greatest revelation of all time. The Spirit is ready to open the eyes and ears of His disciples. They will discern who He is.

Jesus asks the question and Peter gives the answer: the Christ, God's Messiah (Luke 9:20). It is in no way a stretch to believe Christ was interceding in prayer for His disciples before this revelation as Jesus told Peter on another occasion of His intercession for him when Satan demanded to sift him like wheat (Luke 22:31–32). Jesus's prayers brought this revelation of His true identity as the Messiah to Peter.

All followers of Jesus need to discover who He really is. In different circumstances of need we call on God in prayer for help. As we cry out to God, He gives us revelation through the Holy Spirit so that we might understand and experience more of Him. The more we listen to God in times of prayer, the more He reveals His character to us. We discover that our God is omnipotent (having all power), omnipresent (everywhere at the same time), and omniscient (all knowing). We discover He is unsearchable and never-ending.

THE GOOD SHEPHERD

Peter's revelation was so magnificent because it revealed the true character of Jesus, His deity—He is the Son of the living God. Jesus is part of the Godhead, the Trinity. This revelation also revealed Jesus as the long-awaited Messiah, the One who would take away the sins of the world.

"Who do you say Jesus is?" If we answer Messiah, we will find ourselves under the watchful eye of Jehovah-Rohi, the Lord my shepherd. The Good Shepherd watches out for us. He is completely responsible for everything in our lives—our provision, our care, and even our discipline. The character of the Good Shepherd is seen in so many different ways. His watchful eye is on us at all times when we pray for safety. The Good Shepherd orchestrates all things for our good in the midst of troubling circumstances. He even guards us from temptations the enemy brings our way. Jesus said, "I am the good shepherd. The good shepherd lays down His life for the sheep" (John 10:11). The Lord understands us. He knows we long for a sense of security and safety. He reveals Himself as the Good Shepherd, the Lord our shepherd, Jehovah-Rohi as we seek Him in prayer.

> The LORD is my shepherd; I shall not want. He makes me lie down in green pastures; He leads me beside still waters. He restores my soul; He leads me in paths of righteousness for His name's sake. Even though I walk through the valley of the shadow of death, I will fear no evil; for You are with me; Your rod and Your staff, they comfort me. You prepare a table before me in the presence of my enemies; You anoint my head with oil; my cup runs over. Surely goodness and

mercy shall follow me all the days of my life, and I will dwell in the house of the LORD forever.

—PSALM 23

OUR PROVIDER

So often we come to the Lord in prayer for provision—finances and the practical necessities of daily living. In prayer we come to know the identity of God that Abraham discovered in obedience by faith, Jehovah-Jireh, the Lord our provider. When God provided a lamb for the sacrifice in place of Abraham's son Isaac, "Abraham called the name of that place The LORD Will Provide, as it is said to this day, 'In the mount of the LORD it will be provided'" (Gen. 22:14). Abraham understood God didn't merely provide for the sacrifice—He would also provide for the future. In prayer we come to understand that God is our provider both now and always. We can be freed of fear of the future. What a marvelous work of the Holy Spirit this is as we encounter this facet of our Lord's character. By the faith He has given us and by simple prayer, we can live in the revelation that He is Jehovah-Jireh and will always make a way for us.

But my God shall supply your every need according to His riches in glory by Christ Jesus.

—PHILIPPIANS 4:19

THE PRINCE OF PEACE

We know that in prayer Jesus gives us His very best, His presence in our lives. One of the most profound things we can experience in prayer is the peace of Christ. Jesus is the Prince of Peace (Isa. 9:6). The Lord called Gideon to be a valiant warrior, and right in the middle of this call to war Gideon experienced God's peace: "Then Gideon built an altar for the Lord there and called it The Lord Is Peace" (Judg. 6:24). He had an encounter with Jehovah-Shalom, the Lord our peace. By living in a spirit of prayer, we can live in the revelation of God's peace, no matter the circumstance. It doesn't matter how harrowing the battles become; by prayer and faith in God we will live in a spirit of peace. Jehovah-Shalom, the Lord our peace, will be our constant companion.

> Be anxious for nothing, but in everything, by prayer and supplication with gratitude, make your requests known to God. And the peace of God, which surpasses all understanding, will protect your hearts and minds through Christ Jesus.
>
> —Philippians 4:6–7

Our Healer

Our wonderful Savior is the same, yesterday, today, and forever (Heb. 13:8). When we read the Scripture, we see that Jesus healed often, and we can't be anything but convinced that Jesus heals today. There is perhaps no more tangible way that we experience the character of our God than when we experience answered prayer for healing. Yet we see so little of the Lord's healing today. Why is this?

In Exodus 15:26 God revealed Himself as Jehovah-Rapha, the Lord who heals: "If you diligently listen to the voice of the Lord your God, and do what is right in His sight, and give ear to His commandments, and keep all His statutes, I will not afflict you with any of the diseases with which I have afflicted the Egyptians. For I am the Lord who heals you." Notice in this verse that the very first step in healing is to diligently listen to the voice of the Lord. I firmly believe we do not experience the healing character of God because we simply do not know Him well. We do not go to Him in the deep stillness of meditative prayer. We do not listen to and know God our healer or understand His will and ways. As I talk with people, I see the great lack in our land is prayer. We lack the intimacy with our Lord gained only through prayer. But the invitation is open to every one of us. Begin anew today in presenting yourself before the Lord in prayer and the Word and experience this aspect of our God's character, Jehovah-Rapha, the Lord who heals.

> But he was wounded for our transgressions, he was bruised
> for our iniquities; the chastisement of our peace was upon
> him, and by his stripes we are healed.
>
> —ISAIAH 53:5

OUR RIGHTEOUSNESS

Of all the aspects of the Lord's character revealed to us in prayer, this is perhaps the one I rejoice in the most—He is my righteousness. I am a recovering perfectionist, and I entered the Christian life with a warped understanding of work. The answer to all of life's issues had always been to just work harder. Obviously that principle doesn't translate well to the Christian life. Jeremiah prophesied that there would come a day when God would raise up a righteous branch from David and He would be called Jehovah-Tsidkenu, the Lord our Righteousness: "In his days Judah will be saved, and Israel will dwell safely. And this is the name by which he will be called: THE LORD OUR RIGHTEOUSNESS" (Jer. 23:6).

This is what I greatly rejoice in—the Lord has done for me that which I cannot do. I could never be righteous enough to stand before a holy God on my own, but Christ has saved me, and He presents me before the Father clothed in His righteousness. "I will greatly rejoice in the LORD, my soul shall be joyful in my God; for He has clothed me with the garments of salvation, He has covered me with the robe of righteousness, as a bridegroom decks himself with ornaments, and as a bride adorns herself with her jewels" (Isa. 61:10). Thank You, Lord!

> God made Him who knew no sin to be sin for us, that we might become the righteousness of God in Him.
> —2 Corinthians 5:21

Through prayer we can experience the character of our God every morning. Our understanding can be opened to who God really is. That familiarity can last throughout the day and extend through the night hours. The Holy Spirit offers to us the revelation of salvation through the sacrifice of Christ. As we accept Jesus as our Savior and Lord, we have direct access to all that the Father is through prayer.

When You Pray

Prayer opens our understanding of the character of God.

What aspects of the character of God have already been revealed to you?

Do you need a fresh revelation of any of God's character traits? Which ones?

How can the knowledge of the character of God affect your life on a day-to-day basis?

_____

_____

_____

PRAYER CHANGES EVERYTHING

About eight days after these sayings, He took Peter and John and James and went up onto a mountain to pray. As He prayed, the appearance of His countenance was altered, and His clothing was white and glistening.[1]
—LUKE 9:28–29

As HE PRAYED…" While Christ was praying, the appearance of His face became different and He was changed. He was changed! If prayer changed Jesus, what will it do to us? The truth of prayer is this: prayer changes all kind of things; however, the most important change comes in us. Through prayer we can come to God daily, and we can engage our God intimately. The closer we come to God, the more God reveals to us our need to change, and the more we are changed by simply beholding Him.

THE REAL PURPOSE OF PRAYER

Prayer is not easy. It doesn't come naturally. Your natural life may have all the appearance of being vibrant; however, your spiritual life will be atrophied if you don't learn to pray and pray daily. Your relationship with Jesus is nourished and sustained by prayer.

When a person comes to Christ, he or she is born again; a new creation begins in Christ. One of two things happens with this new life we have in Christ. It is either strengthened or it weakens and becomes malnourished. What makes the difference? It is really very simple. We discover strength and intimacy with Christ in the secret place in prayer and the Word. There is a foundation that exists beneath all prayer— a life that is faithful and committed to Jesus. It can't be seized in a moment, but it is available to anyone who is dedicated to following Jesus with his or her whole life.

Prayer changes so many things. Prayer changes your outlook on life. It changes your desires, your loves, your compulsions, and your addictions. It changes you internally and externally. Prayer changes us so that we change things. It is the very nature of prayer to deposit in us the desire to intercede and call down the blessings of God on others.

We think wrongly about prayer for a lot of reasons. Prayer is simply not a part of our natural life; it is communication between our spirit and His Spirit. Our natural, carnal man looks at prayer as foolish and absurd. "The person without the Spirit does not accept the things that come from the Spirit of God but considers them foolishness, and cannot understand them because they are discerned only through the Spirit" (1 Cor. 2:14, NIV). We think prayer is a way to get things. We come to the Lord with our lists, our needs, and our wants. I find that on the whole we ask for requests sporadically. Oh yes, we have the lists that we bring to Him in prayer every now and then, and of course there are the catastrophic events that cast us upon Him. But few people I know come before the Lord every day, throughout the day, petitioning Him to hear requests that will build His kingdom. Everything in our culture points us toward self-sufficiency. Independence is one of the great sins of our day. We do not think we need Him. It is only in humility that we see our genuine state of need that brings us to prayer always and on every occasion.

Why Pray Anyway?

Jesus was always committing things to prayer. Obviously Jesus prayed often; we have twenty-three recorded instances of Jesus praying, and we can assume He prayed on many other occasions. Many times His prayers are dramatic and revealing. They tell us that the great events of His life required intense prayer:

+ Choosing the disciples required all-night prayer.

+ Revealing whom He was to the disciples required devoted time in prayer.

+ The turning point of His time with the disciples and the transition toward the crucifixion required prayer that resulted in a majestic, mysterious interaction with Moses and Elijah.

+ The garden prayers resulted in such agony that Jesus sweat drops of blood, and an angel appeared from heaven to strengthen Him.

When it comes to making life-changing decisions, He set the example for us: seek Him in intense prayer.

Our middle daughter was born three months premature. She had no heartbeat, and the doctors came to my wife and delivered the prognosis: "She is essentially without life, and we question trying to revive her because of the length of time her brain has been without oxygen. If she lives, she will likely have limited brain function." She weighed two pounds and three ounces. Thankfully we were at a Catholic hospital, and they agreed to attempt to revive and save her. Lizzy was in the neonatal intensive care for almost three months. She came home weighing four pounds. Along the way she had just about everything go wrong that could go wrong with a premature baby: breathing issues due to an immature respiratory system, low blood pressure (hypotension), and patent ductus arteriosus (PDA). PDA is a hole in the heart that doesn't close, and for Lizzy it meant heart surgery. Add to that bleeding in the brain, known as an intraventricular hemorrhage, and a gastrointestinal issue called necrotizing enterocolitis (NEC), a condition in which the cells lining the bowel wall are injured and the baby can't process food. My wife and I walked in a spirit of prayer for three months. We were sustained by the day-and-night prayers of so many other believers, and we received a great answer to prayer. Today Liz is an RN and does short-term mission work. Why pray? He answers prayer. And He wants it to be the testimony of our lives.

But what about when the answer from God is "No"? From the mundane things of life we pray for—such as the used car we need for one of our children, the relief we desire from an irritating coworker, or everyday temptations—to the critical situations we face, we need to remind ourselves that our prayers are about His developing His character in our lives and God being glorified through it. We need to remind ourselves of the truth of God's Word: "We also boast in tribulation, knowing that tribulation produces patience, patience produces character, and character produces hope. And hope does not disappoint, because the love of God is shed abroad in our hearts by the Holy Spirit who has been given to us" (Rom. 5:3–5).

HOW DOES GOD CHANGE US?

When it comes to character, God doesn't just give it. And you can't take a class to get character. But as we pray and give ourselves to the Word, we understand how God engineers our circumstances to develop character. He chooses what He allows in our lives, and then He tests us. Character is built when we respond correctly in the right opportunities. He allows for the gamut of character-building circumstances: hardships, temptation, conflict, delays in answered prayer, and so many more.

But what about the sin and strongholds in our lives that we all struggle with? How do we change these? Thank God for His Word and Spirit-empowered prayer. These are the weapons He has given us to tear down strongholds and every high thing that exalts itself against the knowledge of God (2 Cor. 10:3–5; Eph. 6:10–18).

Most people enter the Christian life broken. We have need of emotional and spiritual healing. God has put so many tools at our disposal for restoration. We confess our sins to trusted people and find healing (James 5:16). His Word restores our soul (Ps. 19:7). Whatever the ills we have deep in our soul, Christ promises as we submit to His shepherding, we will find refreshing in our mind, emotions, and will (Ps. 23:2–3). His goal is to save us completely, not just partially: "Therefore he is able to save completely those who come to God through him, because he always lives to intercede for them" (Heb. 7:25, NIV). When He says *completely*, He means 100 percent.

WHEN YOU PRAY

Prayer will change you.

Is change easy or difficult for you?

If it is difficult, what makes you resistant to change? What is one thing you can do about that today?

What are the some of the specific areas in which you need God to change you?

_____

_____

_____

_____

_____

_____

_____

_____

_____

_____

_____

_____

_____

_____

_____

THE MIRACULOUS IN THE MUNDANE

About eight days after these sayings, He took Peter and John and James and went up onto a mountain to pray. As He prayed, the appearance of His countenance was altered, and His clothing was white and glistening.[1]
—LUKE 9:28–29

CHRIST DESIRED TO share this greater mystery and revelation of who He was with Peter, James, and John. He also absolutely desires to share it with us. Jesus used the Transfiguration to display the majestic glory in which we are all privileged to participate—Christ in us, the hope of glory (Col. 1:27).

Jesus maintained His oneness and unity with the Father through prayer. And it is the same for us. Through prayer we will come to know our God and the revelation of His mysteries. It is through prayer that we move into this mysterious oneness with Christ and experience His miraculous power in our life.

Too often we believe that if we answer the call to a particular service, such as being a missionary in a far-off land, we will see miraculous events in our life. Or we have the tendency to think that we must put forth some heroic act to elicit the miraculous. I believe what the transfiguration of Christ reveals to us is that as we pray and seek God, we are changed and the miracles of God slip into our ordinary life. "But we all, seeing the glory of the Lord with unveiled faces, as in a mirror, are being transformed into the same image from glory to glory by the Spirit of the Lord" (2 Cor. 3:18).

The Mundane

What qualifies as miraculous in our everyday mundane lives? It is one thing for us to encounter a great injustice and stay true to God and glorify Him through it as others see our godly character. But what about praying for a coworker's salvation or the success of the place where we work? What about the wife who works and takes care of a home with three kids and a husband and prays for the ability to keep it all together? Are answers to prayer in these situations any less than miraculous? No, they are not.

Flashes of lightning, visions, dreams, revelations, and what we typically view as miraculous aren't daily occurrences for most of us. I believe the Lord does want us to have huge answers to prayer every day and see miracles. That is what I am contending for in my prayer life. Truthfully I am not there. But I am a holding on, and I am putting into proper perspective the miraculous events in my daily life that aren't lightning bolts from heaven.

When we go to work every day, we are plunged into toil and worldly things. The everyday sameness, dreariness, or lack of spirituality at work could cause us to miss what the Lord is doing. The same is true for those who care for children and the home or an elderly parent. But there is a great breakthrough that the Holy Spirit has planned for us. He wants us to experience His miraculous power in the dailiness of life. Prayer is the key to this experience. Prayer can reach beyond what we can see. We can indeed live in an attitude of prayer the entire day, in every conversation and through every task we undertake. And it is through this that the mundane is truly transformed into the miraculous.

But the transformation of prayer can go much deeper. As we face the world every day, we face temptations, and this is where we need the Lord to purify us. Prayer is that act that aligns us with God's purposes in our day. Prayer is the vehicle that frees us from the bondage of flesh. Prayer is our road to transformation. "As he was praying, the appearance of his face changed, and his clothes became as bright as a flash of lightning" (Luke 9:29, NIV).

VISIONS

Yes, visions. All three men, Peter, James, and John, had a simultaneous vision on the mountaintop as they saw the Transfiguration. The whole scene is far beyond our human understanding, frames of reference, or perhaps even imaginations. The truth is we may not even be comfortable with the way God choose to communicate at the Transfiguration. We may unknowingly be trying to limit God in how He can speak to us. However, I promise you that the Lord speaks how He chooses to speak.

I was in the throes of physical failure. The result: daily pain crises that put me in and out of a wheelchair, an opiate addiction, three total knee replacements, and a couple of back surgeries. I sensed the Lord wanted me to quit working. However, I couldn't afford to quit working and couldn't really hear that anyway. Work was all I knew to do; it was the one thing I learned from my dad. If something isn't going well or you need to get ahead, just work harder. That may have been kind of true in the work world, but it did not produce life and peace in me. Worst of all I was deceived into thinking

I could gain God's approval by working harder at being a Christian.

The board of trustees at the Christian academy where I worked was telling me I needed to take a rest, my friends were encouraging me to take a sabbatical, and my wife was encouraging me to use the months of sick leave I had accumulated. Finally I wrote to the Lord in my journal one day, "Lord, if You want me to stop working, You will have to write on the wall, 'You need to quit working.'" I figured if the hand of God wrote it for King Belshazzar (Daniel 5), He could do it for me. Of course, I didn't really believe He would do it. I felt I was safe to keep pressing on. Surely things would improve. But they didn't.

In my desperate physical state I went halfway across the United States for a week of treatment a second time. There I was with a team of doctors and a therapist. They had all my medical files, which at this time were a few inches thick. A new therapist I had never seen before came in. She had evaluated my file and thought she had the answer to my problems. She headed to a huge white board on the wall, wiped it clean, and wrote in big black letters: "YOU NEED TO QUIT WORKING."

Will you open up the realm of possibilities in your life with God through prayer? He wants to dynamite your control, expectations, professionalism, and spiritual dignity. He is on the lookout for a peculiar people. He is inviting you today in prayer to experience this marvelous transformation. "But ye are a chosen generation, a royal priesthood, an holy nation, a peculiar people; that ye should shew forth the praises of him who hath called you out of darkness into his marvellous light" (1 Pet. 2:9, KJV). Now that is transformation.

WHEN YOU PRAY

In prayer we discover the miraculous in the mundane.

What is the most seemingly boring and spiritually unproductive facet of your life? Ask the Holy Spirit to work the miraculous in the mundane of your life and give you spiritual eyes to see it.

_____

_____

_____

_____

_____

_____

_____

_____

_____

_____

_____

_____

_____

_____

_____

HIDDEN THINGS

*At that time Jesus prayed this prayer: "O Father, Lord of heaven
and earth, thank you for hiding these things from those who
think themselves wise and clever, and for revealing them to the
childlike. Yes, Father, it pleased you to do it this way!"* [1]
—MATTHEW 11:25–26, NLT

JESUS PRAYED AND gave thanksgiving to the Father. Why?
Because the disciples had ministered with authority. Jesus
rejoiced in the Holy Spirit for the reason that these simple
men, mere babes in the faith, had demonstrated that which
prophets and kings had waited to see, the power of the gospel
in action.

WHO ARE THESE PEOPLE?

In this particular prayer Jesus spoke of things that were
hidden from the wise and clever—those who thought themselves wise, according to what the world says is wise. Paul
puts it this way, "Brothers and sisters, think of what you
were when you were called. Not many of you were wise by
human standards; not many were influential; not many were
of noble birth. But God chose the foolish things of the world
to shame the wise; God chose the weak things of the world
to shame the strong" (1 Cor. 1:26–27, NIV). So the people
Paul speaks of are the wise by human standards, the influential, and the nobility.

The wise by human standards

The wise by human standards are those who take pride in their educational or philosophical attainments. They accumulate knowledge, but the true nature of the gospel eludes many of them. They have licenses, bachelor degrees, master degrees, divinity degrees, theology degrees, and doctorates, ad infinitum. They glory in the prestigious institutions they have attended. Their studies include exegesis, logic, expository preaching, eschatology, and hermeneutics. They know the original Hebrew and Greek. Too often they are the ones of whom Paul spoke about to Timothy, "always learning, but never able to come to the knowledge of the truth" (2 Tim. 3:7). Paul could speak directly to this from experience. He was numbered in this lot.

The wise by human standards seem to be disciples. They put themselves under the umbrella of Christian organizations and educational institutions. They are professional, religious teachers, but they never acquire the true knowledge of the way of salvation. "You shall know the truth, and the truth shall set you free" (John 8:32). The truth? Jesus.

The wise become intimate with the "doctrines" of Christianity but never accept Christ as their Savior. They study church history but remain strangers to the fellowship of the saints today. They are philosophers but never become personally familiar with the Holy Spirit. Our religious denominations and institutions are full of religious people who do not know Jesus.

Don't take my prose as an indictment on theological education or education in general. I am a lifelong educator and have worked as an administrator at a Christian university, a principal in secular high schools, and a Christian school headmaster. However, it is clear we overvalue education when it comes to knowing Christ, serving Him, and having the power of the Holy Spirit in prayer. We automatically equate theological education with spirituality and wisdom; they do not necessarily connect. In many religious circles advanced educational degrees are the first qualification for leadership rather than godly wisdom or a person's prayer life.

One of my dearest lifelong friends is at the national leadership level in his denomination. He is a passionate follower of Jesus and a man of prayer. To reach his level of leadership required numerous degrees, years of overseas advanced study at one of the most prestigious seminaries in the world, continual "professional development," and regular attendance at required yearly conferences. In a conversation with him after he completed seminary education, he reminisced about the many faculty members under whose tutelage he sat. Though they were learned professors of theology, he observed that only a couple of them displayed the character of a person who knew and served Christ intimately.

The influential

The influential are men and women of success, CEOs, company presidents, entrepreneurs, lawyers, doctors, politicians, and businesspeople. They are those who epitomize achievement by the world's standards. They are the influential who dominate the leadership boards of Christian schools and universities, seminaries, churches, and denominations. If they have an interest in spiritual matters, other Christians often assume they have godly wisdom that corresponds to their worldly wisdom and that they know something of the power of prayer. While these bright, influential, and gifted people bring needed perceptiveness and acumen to religious enterprises, they do not always bring the same depth of spiritual leadership or intimacy with Jesus that is gained only though prayer.

The nobility

The nobility are the highest class in society. They are people of royalty, privilege, and reputation. They are those who are born to wealth, including many politicians, the highest governing officials, the aristocracy, and others. These people are welcomed into positions of spiritual leadership because they bring with them notoriety, prestige, and a corresponding level of influence. But simply put, they often lack the depth of relationship with Jesus to add any spiritual value in leadership.

The wise, the influential, and the nobility—some of the greatest scholars, most influential statesmen, and most noble—have been the greatest strangers to the gospel. The world's wisdom does not lead one to know God's wisdom. "For since, in the wisdom of God, the world through its wisdom did not know God, it pleased God through the foolishness of preaching to save those who believe" (1 Cor. 1:21). The truth is that those who are the experts in the secular can be the least experienced in the realms of the Spirit. For want of an experience of the saving power of Jesus Christ, a person may dive deeply into the mysteries of nature and the administration of state, and yet be ignorant of and/or mistaken about the mysteries and administration of the kingdom of heaven.

TRUE WISDOM

My sphere of association is somewhat limited; nonetheless, I have had occasion to relate to a wide variety of people. I am sure there are many spiritually wise and godly people I have missed along the way. However, two of the wisest and godly men I know are deeply connected to Jesus through prayer. They know the power of prayer in the Holy Spirit.

Lattie did not finish junior high. When I met him, he was in his early fifties and working at a trucking company as a dispatcher. The demands of ministry drew him into full-time travel, preaching the Word and encouraging churches through to his eighties. He ministered in many foreign countries and almost all states in the United States. He quietly mentored men who are nationally recognized leaders in the body of Christ today. If I mentioned their names here, you would recognize many of them. I say "quietly" because he never drew attention to himself. He didn't advertise, do direct mail, or have a brand. Lattie is a combination of humility, kindness, spiritual authority, and childlikeness. His wisdom is unending. His discernment is almost mystical. His ministry of the Word is inspiring. He is the wisest man I know.

Joe was a high school dropout. He spent twenty-plus years as a drug dealer and user of almost every type of illegal drug. From flying drugs across the US border to being the "bag man" for cities, Joe's life was absorbed by the drug culture. He eventually ended up in prison and was in his forties before being dramatically saved. Today Joe walks in heavenly humility and with a spiritual authority that is astounding. He wins people to Christ, and he encourages everyone he speaks to. Because he knows the depth of the Lord's forgiveness, Joe's simplicity, boldness, and passion are infectious. A walking miracle, Joe has been healed twice of serious cancer. During his last bout of cancer treatment I chauffeured him for a few days. It seemed like I had shadowed one of Jesus's twelve disciples. Simple, trusting, vulnerable, and loving to all, Joe is childlike but full of godly wisdom and authority. When he speaks, people stop and listen.

Yes, the things concerning Jesus and the Father are hidden from the wise and clever and revealed to those with childlike faith, those who have come to know an intimacy with the Father that is only gained in the secret place of prayer. Jesus Christ said, "Unless you...become like little children..." (Matt. 18:3).

WHEN YOU PRAY

God reveals hidden things to those with childlike faith.

Would you characterize your growth in the wisdom of the Lord as static or dynamic? Why?

What part do you think wisdom should play in your prayer life?

Ask the Holy Spirit to show you how to grow in spiritual wisdom.

For further study see 1 Samuel 2:26; Luke 2:52; Colossians 2:2–3; James 1:5; 3:17.

HUMILITY BRINGS
ENDLESS POSSIBILITIES

At that time Jesus prayed this prayer: "O Father, Lord of heaven
and earth, thank you for hiding these things from those who
think themselves wise and clever, and for revealing them to the
childlike. Yes, Father, it pleased you to do it this way!"[1]
—MATTHEW 11:25–26, NLT

EDUCATION IS SUCH a two-edged sword. Clearly we need education to survive and thrive in our information-hungry world. The axiom is ever true—education is power. But as powerful as education is for us, it is just as perilous to our spiritual lives.

THE PRIDE PROBLEM

We have a problem, and it is called pride. It is sinister and lurks around the corner of every success and attainment in life. The more educated we are, the greater the temptation to be proud, contemptuous, and even arrogant. These temptations are so subtle, yet if realized, they destroy the spiritual life. There are those with the ability to manage their educational achievements and remain humble, broken, and needy before the Lord. However, too often advanced degrees and titles, particularly those related to theology, become status symbols. Even more devastating is the fleshly tendency for educational attainment to become the essence of a person's identity. What's the safeguard to becoming puffed up with knowledge? It is a corresponding deeper love that flows from intimacy with Christ that is gained in prayer. "Knowledge produces arrogance, but love edifies" (1 Cor. 8:1).

Humility is recognizing that most of your personal success is due to the investment that others have made in you—your parents, teachers, mentors, spouse, friends, bosses, coworkers, pastors, etc. So many people touch our lives in a deep, positive way. You see this kind of humility in the life of Jesus. He honored the Father. He wanted the Father to be glorified through His life. This humility is how Jesus describes Himself: "Take my yoke upon you and learn from me, for I am gentle and humble in heart, and you will find rest for your souls" (Matt. 11:29, NIV).

Our Lord's humility is apparent in everything He does; it is His nature, His Spirit. Jesus's first response upon hearing of the disciples' triumphant return was to praise the Father and rejoice in the Holy Spirit. What an amazing response. His first thought was thankfulness to the Father for revealing all of these things to the disciples. Jesus attributes all to the Father. He directs all honor, praise, and glory to the Father, never mind that He has essentially spent three years with the disciples day and night.

What is your first response to the success of someone else? I believe that the undeniable proof of unity is when you see people get excited about the success of others. In my years of working with young people, facilitating unity has been a personal goal. Seeing young people care for one another and support one another is a beautiful thing. I believe a unique and blessed experience of unity is attained when people are excited about the success of others.

What is your immediate response to personal success?

Do your thoughts move to those who invested in you, those who sacrificed to bring you to this joyous position? Read the words of Jesus as He speaks of His relationship with the Father. When He speaks of Himself, notice the words He uses: *not* and *nothing*.

+ "Truly, truly I say to you, the Son can do nothing of Himself, but what He sees the Father do. For whatever He does, likewise the Son does" (John 5:19).

+ "I can do nothing of Myself. As I hear, I judge. My judgment is just, because I seek not My own will, but the will of the Father who sent Me" (John 5:30).

+ "I do not receive honor from men" (John 5:41).

+ "My teaching is not Mine, but His who sent Me" (John 7:16).

+ "You know Me and you likewise know where I am from. I have not come on My own authority, but He who sent Me is true, whom you do not know" (John 7:28).

+ "When you lift up the Son of Man, then you will know that I am He, and I do nothing of Myself. But I speak these things as My Father taught Me" (John 8:28).

+ "I do not seek glory for Myself. There is One who seeks it and judges" (John 8:50).

+ "Do you not believe that I am in the Father and the Father is in Me? The words that I say to you I do not speak on My own authority. But the Father who lives in Me does the works" (John 14:10).

+ "He who does not love Me does not keep My words.
The word which you hear is not Mine, but the
Father's who sent Me" (John 14:24).

When it comes to Christ's humility, these scriptures are
convincing. They make humility a great deal more tangible.
They bring to life the scripture, "[Christ Jesus], being in the
form of God, did not consider equality with God something to be grasped. But He emptied Himself, taking upon
Himself the form of a servant, and was made in the likeness
of men" (Phil. 2:6–7).

Jesus opens up before us a heavenly humility. With this
humility comes endless possibilities in prayer.

SERVICE OR RELATIONSHIP

It is not service that our Lord is after; it is relationship. The
pitfall we fall into is to "rejoice" in how God has used us or
to seek the approval of others through service. If you are
walking with Him daily, then He will pour His life through
you, whatever you experience, whomever you encounter. You
will know what it is to pray and receive answers to prayer.
Others will be blessed as you walk in obedience.

Here's the truth of the matter—we come to know our
Lord through prayer. Prayer is the key to intimacy. The Lord
approves of our desires to serve Him and of our pursuits to
study and know the Word. But that is not what He is after
in our lives. He wants us to come and deeply commune with
Him in the quiet place. He looks at our lives, our characters,
and our personalities. Christ sees what we can look like completed in Him, the beauty of it all. He ever invites us into the
secret place to know Him as a little child, setting aside our

experiences, our pride, our education, our degrees, and our achievements.

He speaks to us, "I love you, My little child. Walk closely to Me so that you can draw upon Me quickly. You can always speak to Me through prayer."

Dear saints, our world doesn't need deeper revelation, a greater proliferation of dynamic sermons, or a clearer definition of the gospel. We do not need more men and women of intense, advanced theological education. We need those who have power in prayer. What the world is waiting on is a demonstration of the power of the Holy Spirit.

When You Pray

Humility brings your words, actions, and prayers in line with the will of the Father.

What are the positions in life or achievements that define your identity? How would you feel and what would you do if these "identifiers" were removed from your life?

_____

_____

_____

_____

_____

_____

PRAYING LIKE A CHILD

*Then little children were brought to Him that He might
put His hands on them and pray. But the disciples rebuked
them. But Jesus said, "Let the little children come to Me, and
do not forbid them. For to such belongs the kingdom of heaven."
He laid His hands on them and departed from there.*[1]
—MATTHEW 19:13–15

THERE IS NO second-guessing about what we must be like
to enter the kingdom of heaven. There is no test to pass
to see if we have reached the right score on the righteousness
scale. There is no spiritual timepiece to measure the
minimum requirement for prayer and Bible study. There are
no quotas on the number of people we must win to the Lord.
There is only one required standard to enter the kingdom of
heaven: childlike faith in Christ as Savior.

THE KINGDOM OF HEAVEN
BELONGS TO SUCH AS THESE

Jesus said, "Let the little children come to Me, and do not
forbid them. For to such belongs the kingdom of heaven"
(Matt. 19:14). What are the characteristics of little children
that impact the faith that we need to enter the kingdom?

Simplicity in living

One of the enviable characteristics of children is that they
are simple. A little child is perfectly happy with socks that
don't match or a shirt with a tear. Children can walk around

with their hair uncombed or smears of food or dirt on their faces and be completely at ease. They aren't into designer clothes and accessories unless they are taught to be. When they have people in their lives pouring blessings and praise on them, telling them how beautiful and exceptional they are, and loving them unconditionally, they are perfectly secure. It is miraculous how little children who aren't getting this kind of care can still exhibit childlike simplicity. It comes naturally. The part of the brain or psyche that rises and falls on what others think hasn't been awakened in little children.

I am experiencing the wonder of having grandchildren. Oh, what fun it is. One of my daughters named our first granddaughter Cameron. I am completely ruined. I get to see Cameron every day and twice on a good day. Our grandson, Isaac, is one year older than Cameron and was the first grandchild on both sides of the family. You can imagine all of the stuff he received. But when the dust had settled after three years and countless toys, his favorite plaything was a huge box. It was a big, old hot tub box that he and granny Annie painted, cut windows and a door in, and decorated. You could see it in Cameron's eyes as she grew; she was drooling (literally) with envy until the day she could crawl into *the* box.

Both those little kids set aside the state-of-the-art, brain-training-based, and developmentally appropriate toys that had all the bells, whistles, flashing lights, and voice synthesized stimulus in favor of a plain cardboard box. Those two children would leave behind a digital, flashing, vibrating toy phone for a wooden spoon and a pot. It really doesn't take a great deal of stimulus and gadgetry to make a child happy. What does it take to make you happy and put a smile on your face? What prayer does God need to answer to make you satisfied?

Expectations, complexity, and busyness have become the American way of life. The expectations of being a good parent and provider and the bombardment of information through media and the Internet are two of the most prevalent things that lead to the complications and hurriedness in our lives. The multitasking lifestyle of today seems to lead to this unsurprising conclusion for most Christians: we're too busy to pray.

Conversely it seems children can live very spartanly and be quite happy. Little Isaac's mom and dad are doctors and are training him to eat all foods and drink water. It is fascinating and unusual to see a little child drink water and be happy. However, I think almost all children are healthier and just as satisfied with water until they are introduced to our addictive, sugar-saturated, placating drinks. Our Lord gave us a very simple prescription for prayer in our daily living. He said to pray for daily provision, to be able to live in forgiveness, and to be freed from temptation and the evil one. Yes, prayer can be very simple.

Simply accepting others

Little children are harmless and inoffensive. They are meek, free from malice, and without pride. Little children do not have ambitious ideas or desires for superiority. Little children act as if everyone is equal. Little children are not prejudiced. They may notice color, but it makes no difference to them. Where do you go to school? How much money does your parent make? How big is your house? These are all questions that wouldn't cross a child's mind.

Thursday of every week is my day to take four-year-old

Isaac to a popular chicken place. It serves food that is healthy to a degree and provides a great indoor play place. It never fails—within a few minutes of playing, he has made friends with other little kids, and they are transformed into lifelong buds. Nearly every time one of the kids he is playing with leaves or we go, it is like he is having his best friend ripped out of his life. He is a little dramatic; nonetheless, what has taken place is very real to him. He has made friends quickly. Children accept others as they are. They don't judge, size up, scrutinize, evaluate, or compare. Little kids only know friends, not acquaintances, colleagues, or strangers—only friends. They just play well with others. Do you play well with others?

Contentment

There are numerous synonyms for *contentment*: *satisfaction*, *gratification*, or *happiness*. All of these words identify something about children that is so Christlike: the ability to be grateful or satisfied with today. I recently had a discussion with a group of people about the topic, "What does it look like to be childlike?" One thought rose to the top: not being concerned about tomorrow. Jesus taught His disciples much about this idea on a number of occasions. Here is just one: "Therefore do not worry about tomorrow, for tomorrow will worry about itself. Each day has enough trouble of its own" (Matt. 6:34, NIV). What a scandalous thought! Could Jesus have really meant what He said?

Not worrying about tomorrow is a marvelous challenge, and what great freedom it would bring. Can you imagine being able to live in the moment? The thought of it rankles against everything in our culture. We are always preparing and thinking about tomorrow, looking at our to-do list, and setting appointments. Being childlike brings with it the freedom to slow down, stop for just one person, and see the stunning value of every child of God.

I am convinced that this childlikeness is the only position that will bring us the freedom to slow down and let prayer permeate the depths of our lives throughout the day. Prayer and busyness are like oil and water. They simply don't mix well. Every one of us has limitations. We have a maximum capacity or limit on our bandwidth, if you will. Busyness is like video streaming to the bandwidth of our souls (mind, emotions, and will). Busyness devours the soul's bandwidth and leaves no room for prayer to run on the communication highway to God.

When You Pray

Childlikeness removes hindrances to prayer.

Is there a particular area of your life in which you are experiencing a lack of peace or that occupies a disproportionate amount of your thoughts? Make a plan this week to share this with a trusted friend and ask for prayer.

_____

_____

_____

_____

_____

_____

FAITH LIKE A CHILD

Then little children were brought to Him that He might
put His hands on them and pray. But the disciples rebuked
them. But Jesus said, "Let the little children come to Me, and
do not forbid them. For to such belongs the kingdom of heaven."
He laid His hands on them and departed from there.[1]
—MATTHEW 19:13–15

THERE IS SOMETHING nourishing in love and acceptance that is initiated by touch. Few things compare to tactile expressions of intimacy: the gentle brush of a lover's hand across your cheek to express tender affection; the consoling pat on the back from a dear friend; or the loving embrace of a mom or dad. Intimacy brings great emotional fulfillment and release to our souls. There is a mystical, dynamic connection that exists between intimacy and touch. It is almost as though intimacy is fulfilled in a soft, untainted touch. In intimacy we are known. In it we risk and come out of hiding. Prayer is intimacy with our Lord.

INTIMACY

Annamae, my wife, has numerous deep-hearted relationships with other women and pours her life into others. More than anyone I know, she understands the subtle nuances of friendship: listening, availability, reminders of friendship, and the investment of time, to mention a few. Through raising and homeschooling our children, Annamae coined an expression about intimacy that has become our truism in relationships: "Intimacy breaks rebellion." Intimacy in relationships tears down walls of secrecy, obliterates bastions of privacy, and invades the asylum of loneliness. Intimacy can have many expressions, such as time spent listening, an encouraging word or note, or an unexpected gift. However, nothing compares with a tender touch.

Intimacy is yielding to the Holy Spirit, allowing the Holy Spirit to view every corridor of our hearts. Then it is looking deeply into the Lord in the secret place of quietness and stillness before Him. It is in intimacy with Jesus through prayer that our capacity for intimacy with others is deepened.

When I visited India a few years ago, one of the striking differences in culture I noticed was men holding hands as an expression of friendship. While walking around, I saw many male friends holding hands or with an arm draped around their friend's neck. Obviously, in our homophobic society holding the hand of a dear male friend or having your arm around his neck is not generally considered to be an option. I give many of my close male friends a hug every now and then; however, it has an awkward, embarrassing feel to it. The awkwardness I feel is a reflection of our cultural norms wherein a man doesn't express affection toward another man. We have turned so many aspects of relationships upside down in our godless culture. Perhaps this is another example of just that.

Jesus desired to lay hands on the children and pray for them. Oh, how different our world would be today if fathers laid their hands on their children and prayed for them. Nothing is more powerful, yet loving and tender, than a father laying his hands on his children and blessing them. Whether it is a child of two or twelve, touch and prayer foster intimacy. Intimacy breaks rebellion. It paves the way for relationship.

In the Gospel of Luke the chronicle of the same encounter with Jesus uses the word *infants* rather than *children* (Luke

18:15). It is probably for this reason that the disciples rebuked those who brought the children, thinking that they were too young to receive any benefit from the encounter with Christ. Even so, Christ says the kingdom of heaven belongs to such as these. There is no other stage in our lives when we are more helpless and dependent than when we are infants. Like lambs we need a caretaker—a shepherd—to care for us.

> *Lord Jesus, open our eyes to see our helplessness to enter the kingdom unless we become like little children utterly dependent on You. Let us be as dependent upon You as You were dependent on the Father.*

POOR IN SPIRIT

Can an educated, seasoned man have faith like a little child? Can a mature, sophisticated woman learn to trust like a little child? In our culture we are taught to be independent. Autonomy is prized and longed for. In the midst of all this self-sufficiency, accumulation of stuff, professionalism, entrepreneurship, and status seeking, is it possible for us to recognize our great need? No matter our education or our wealth, we are helpless to enter Christ's kingdom unless we become desperate and needy for our Savior. And our need is endless, whether we recognize it or not. We must constantly turn to God in prayer as a little child runs to her parents. The poor in spirit are those who recognize their great need for Jesus. "Blessed are the poor in spirit, for theirs is the kingdom of heaven" (Matt. 5:3).

Is it possible for a man or woman, no matter what age or status, to become childlike again? Nicodemus said to Christ that surely a man couldn't enter into his mother's womb a second time to be born. Of course, when Jesus spoke of being born again, He was speaking of a spiritual birth (John 3:3–7). All things are possible through the power of the Holy Spirit.

The question you must ask yourself is: Do I really trust my heavenly Father the way a little child trusts? Your prayers will reveal your belief system when it comes to trust in the Father. You see, I really do believe my heavenly Father is loving and faithful and has my best interests at heart. I believe He hears my prayers. I believe God the Father looks at me as one of His little children. He calls me up close to Him and says, "Tell Me what is on your heart, son." He says, "Get quiet and listen to what I say to you."

So simple, so conversational, so unprofessional, so real. That's the way He teaches us to pray. He desires the honest simplicity of praying like a little child, not praying to be heard by others or attempting to impress God. Now there is an outlandish thought. Can you imagine trying to impress God with your prayers? What a waste of time.

In coming to our Lord in prayer with the spirit of child-likeness, we will realize the Fatherhood of God in our lives.

WHEN YOU PRAY

Faith like a child brings intimacy with the Father.

Ask the Holy Spirit to reveal to you a few steps you can take this week to be intentional about a more childlike relationship with your heavenly Father.

_____

_____

_____

Day 22

PRAYING WITH BOLDNESS

So they took away the stone from the place where the dead man was lying. Jesus lifted up His eyes and said, "Father, I thank You that You have heard Me. I know that You always hear Me. But because of the people standing around, I said this, that they may believe that You sent Me." When He had said this, He cried out with a loud voice, "Lazarus, come out!" He who was dead came out, his hands and feet wrapped with grave clothes, and his face wrapped with a cloth.[1]
—JOHN 11:41–44

WHERE DO YOU begin in the life of prayer, and in particular where do you go to learn to pray? It is something I appreciate about this journey of discovery about prayer—Jesus has put a well-defined pathway before us. It is not hidden. The pathway is revealed clearly in His Word. Jesus wants us to see the way. Set your course with these scriptures:

+ "You will make known to me the path of life; in Your presence is fullness of joy; at Your right hand there are pleasures for evermore" (Ps. 16:11).

+ "Enter at the narrow gate, for wide is the gate and broad is the way that leads to destruction, and there are many who are going through it, because small is the gate and narrow is the way which leads to life, and there are few who find it" (Matt. 7:13–14).

+ "Jesus said to him, 'I am the way, the truth, and the life. No one comes to the Father except through Me'" (John 14:6).

Taking the First Step

The famous philosopher, baseball player Yogi Berra, once said, "When you come to a fork in the road, take it."[2] Right now we are on a spiritual journey to understand prayer more clearly by looking deeply into the way Jesus prayed. Every day in this journey we are confronted with distractions, side-tracks, U-turns, off-ramps, and even roadblocks. It is critically important to choose the correct path on this journey. No matter where you are in life, you can take the correct fork. The course you take will be the future direction for all your spiritual efforts and prayers. Take the right course, and it creates the greatest efficiency with your energy and resources. Take the wrong fork in the road, and you will waste your most dynamic, yet limited, resource—time.

What is the most important step to take right now about prayer? I believe it is to be deeply convinced that the Lord hears your prayers. It is the decision I remind myself of almost every time I set my course to pray. I always quote a few of the scriptures that promise the Father hears my prayers to start my prayer time.

+ "I will do whatever you ask in My name, that the Father may be glorified in the Son. If you ask anything in My name, I will do it" (John 14:13–14).

+ "You did not choose Me, but I chose you, and appointed you, that you should go and bear fruit, and that your fruit should remain, that the Father may give you whatever you ask Him in My name" (John 15:16).

+ "On that day you will ask Me nothing. Truly, truly I say to you, whatever you ask the Father in My name, He will give it to you" (John 16:23).

Dare to Be Bold

When the disciples first chose to follow Jesus, they were ignorant concerning the power of prayer. They knew nothing about the power that would become theirs as they prayed in His name. However, Jesus made it profoundly clear as the end of His time on earth drew near: abide in Him, ask in His name, and discover the power to pray in the Holy Spirit. They could unite in prayer with the Holy Spirit and see more magnificent answers to prayer than one could ever dream.

Jesus's prayer for Lazarus was indeed a bold prayer. You may think, "He was Jesus. Of course *He* could pray for someone to be raised from the dead." Yet here is the absolute truth! "At that time you won't need to ask me for anything. I tell you the truth, you will ask the Father directly, and he will grant your request because you use my name" (John 16:23, NLT).

Anything?

Dr. Alan Holderness, a medical doctor I have known for many years, assumed his wife, Jan, was having the onset of a stroke first thing that Saturday. He knew it was serious. He immediately took her to the ER, where she deteriorated quickly. The CT scan showed what looked like a tumor or an aneurism at the base of the brain, large and intrusive. Alan viewed it himself. Jan progressed to an unresponsive state and developed paralysis on the left side of her body. Her blood pressure was very high, and then she had a serious seizure. At 3:00 p.m. the ER team reported they didn't know whether she would survive, and if she did, her quality of life would be poor at best. The doctors asked Alan to call the family in as soon as possible. Prayer requests were sent out everywhere.

Then the ER doctor said there was no treatment available.

The family was told the doctors doubted she would survive, and by late afternoon she was sent to neuro-ICU with little hope. This all transpired in less than one day.

From the time Jan went to the ER, God had put on the hearts of her doctor husband and daughter-in-law to pray Psalm 118:17 that says, "I will not die but live, and will proclaim what the LORD has done" (NIV). They obeyed the prompting of the Lord and prayed with boldness. At 5:00 p.m. their daughter Anne, a pastor's wife, called from Nashville. After hearing about the situation, she said, "Dad, she will not die but live. God had impressed on me last Wednesday to pray for you and mom Psalm 118:17."

There was no change in Jan at 6:00 p.m., and the situation was dire. By this time the family had arrived and were praying with all their hearts. Jan was still unresponsive, but she began stabilizing. On Sunday they did an MRI to further define the lesion in brain. It was gone—everything was gone! The doctors repeated the MRI on Monday with the same findings; there was nothing there. Alan himself saw the MRIs that showed the lesion/aneurism before and its disappearance after. There was no explanation except the Lord had healed Jan. By Sunday evening she was not only better but was sitting up in a chair as the family gathered in her hospital room to praise and worship Jesus. Jan sang also. She left the hospital a few days later.

If we are assured that our heavenly Father hears our prayers, then we will pray over all things. We will pray with boldness. We will pray prayers that are scandalous to the mind, outlandish in enormity, and boundless in their answered impact on our lives. Our faith will be jettisoned to a new level, and we will "come boldly to the throne of grace, that we may obtain mercy and find grace to help in time of need" (Heb. 4:16, NKJV).

Does this mean that God is like a genie in a lamp who grants our every wish? Of course not. But because we have this assurance that our Father hears our prayers, we do not have to question why prayers are seemingly not answered or there is a delay in the answer. Our Father is good, kind, and loving, and He is completely, without question, trustworthy. He is always at work, even in the things we do not see. He is still at work in the unseen, the eternal. So be bold in your prayers. Go boldly before the throne to find grace to help in your times of need.

WHEN YOU PRAY

Knowing God hears allows you to pray with boldness.

Dare today to pray for great answers to your prayers.

Write down your great requests in prayer this week, persevere in prayer, and revisit these prayers often. Chronicle the date you prayed and the date your prayer is answered. You will see mighty answers to prayer.

_____

_____

_____

_____

_____

DAY 23

EXPECT PANCAKES

So they took away the stone from the place where the dead man was lying. Jesus lifted up His eyes and said, "Father, I thank You that You have heard Me. I know that You always hear Me. But because of the people standing around, I said this, that they may believe that You sent Me." When He had said this, He cried out with a loud voice, "Lazarus, come out!" He who was dead came out, his hands and feet wrapped with grave clothes, and his face wrapped with a cloth.[1]
—JOHN 11:41–44

WE HAVE LEARNED that Jesus had set times of prayer, but He also prayed on every occasion. It was as if Jesus was constantly walking around knowing that the Father was near. He and the Father were always listening to each other, communing, and communicating. Then on particular occasions, such as this one, Jesus would verbalize His prayers so others could hear He was praying. Praying without ceasing was His example.

It raises one of the most important questions we can ask ourselves about our spiritual life: How is my prayer life? Is it continual, or is it erratic? Whatever it is like, He wants to blast away any hindrances to prayer.

BLOWING THE LID OFF

The incident of Lazarus's being raised from the dead speaks volumes about Jesus's prayer life. His prayer was bold and public. He wasn't afraid to ask for something big. James 4:2 says, "You do not have, because you do not ask." So Jesus asked. His prayer and the raising of Lazarus blew the lid off all the limitations of propriety and pessimism and opened up a world of possibilities.

PROPRIETY

Jesus had the men roll away the stone of a tomb where Lazarus had been for four days. Martha was trying to process the whirlwind of events taking place around her. Her brother had died, and now Jesus was there, four days later. Realizing the impropriety, the stark reality of disturbing her brother's grave, she just blurted out, "Lord, by this time he stinketh" (John 11:39, KJV). But Jesus wasn't concerned about propriety.

Following Jesus and praying continually can put us in some very uncomfortable situations. We discover ourselves in the middle of events that question our respectability, reputation, and even decency.

I was standing in the dressing room at the gym in my towel, getting ready to get dressed. I had just finished a swim. A man walked in who was obviously very stressed. His buddy came right behind him. The man was continually cursing loudly, using the Lord's name in vain. It was a very large dressing room, but they came to the locker next to me. They searched everything they could get their hands on—a locker, clothes, and his gym bag. (I noticed the hole torn in his bag.) Obviously he had lost something very important, and I assumed it was his keys.

The Lord gifts us in many different and unusual ways. One of my peculiar propensities has been to pray to find lost billfolds or keys and sometimes see immediate answers. I've had some of the most hilarious and inspiring results. I thought,

"Why not?" So I asked the fellow if I could just say a prayer that we find his keys. He responded, "OK." I said a short prayer and asked the Lord to help us find those keys. It got quiet, and he looked me in the eyes as I was standing there in my towel, less than a yard from him. He was silent for about five seconds, which seemed like five minutes to me. Then he responded, "Thank You, Lord. Thank You, Jesus. My keys are attached to my ID card that I left out front when I checked in. Thank You, Lord." I simply replied, "Thank You, Lord."

PESSIMISM

For all those pessimists out there, we have Thomas, the eternal pessimist. He had difficulty believing almost anything. His words reeked of unbelief. Thomas knew Jesus would not be dissuaded from going to Judea, where their lives would be in danger. Jesus had set His mind to go there. Thomas gives one of the most absolute, pessimistic statements recorded in the Scriptures: "Let us go also, that we may die with Him" (John 11:16). Yet Jesus destroyed pessimism. Not only did the disciples not die, but also Jesus raised Lazarus from the dead. Oh, and many of the Jews who had come to visit Mary saw what Jesus did and believed in Him. There you go, pessimist.

If you want to have your pessimism about answered prayer dealt a deathblow, just give the Lord a chance. Wait on Him to guide your thoughts in what to pray. Read the scriptures over again about Jesus's hearing your prayers. Write down your prayers, and revisit them daily. You will see answers to prayer, and your pessimism will fade away in light of miraculous answers.

Pessimism in prayer can even be pulverized by pancakes.

Before a mission trip to Peru a mission team constantly talked about increasing its capacity for the things of God. A young man on the team had always heard of crazy events happening, but he had never witnessed or experienced them. Before they got on the plane to Peru, he got out his notebook and jotted down his expectations. Of course he put down spiritual things: salvations, blind people seeing, and healings like never before.

He decided to add things he enjoyed to the list as well, including Reese's Peanut Butter Cups and pancakes. The young man had always had this thing about pancakes, wanting to try them in different places he traveled. After he finished his list, he wrote, "God will meet my expectations and more." Shortly after he put away his list, a teammate offered him a Reese's Peanut Butter Cup. God came through! He checked one thing off his list.

Every night in Peru they worshipped and talked about the experiences of the day. They heard about many people accepting and proclaiming Jesus as their Lord and Savior. On the fourth night one of the girls on the team shared a story of a person with a horrible eye disease. No matter what pair of glasses she tried, nothing helped the woman see. After a team member prayed for the woman, her face lit up with delight—she said she could see perfectly! From that moment on the team heard of many other people saying they were healed of arthritis and back ailments, not to mention all the hearts that were restored.

On the last day the mission team had a recap meeting. The young man was thinking of all the amazing things God had done and how He had met almost all the young man's expectations. He thought, "Even if I don't get pancakes, I'm in awe of God. He blew past my expectations." As they were packing up and getting ready to leave, the mother of the house asked, "Who wants pancakes?" The young man froze. He was completely speechless. He was about to eat pancakes in Peru. God had met all his expectations. God is always faithful to come through. God reminded him that if you expect it, you will receive it. Our God always exceeds expectations.

Possibilities

Oh, the possibilities in prayer. From people being raised from the dead or healed to children speaking out the things of the Lord and miraculous encounters in daily life, so many great answers to prayer are possible. Following Jesus is the adventure of adventures. The lid blew off as the stone rolled away. Nothing is impossible with God (Luke 1:37)—not even Peruvian pancakes.

Here is the driving reality of prayer: we can pray and see people healed, lives changed, and the lost found. We can see great answers and small answers to prayer. I believe the small answers to prayer can be every bit as impactful. Seeing small, seemingly insignificant answers to prayer will boost our faith and cause us to pray about all things. And in so doing, we will begin to live in a spirit of prayer. The answers to prayer will always be coming.

When You Pray

Answers to prayer are limited by your lack of expectation.

Take a risk today and in the days to come—pray over the simplest things. Persevere in prayer throughout the day, and be mindful of the small challenges you face and the minor decisions you make.

Answer this question after a few days: Did I sense the "spirit of prayer" more in my life?

If you did and you desire to have that spirit of prayer in operation in your life, write a short prayer to the Holy Spirit and invite Him into your every day.

_____

_____

_____

_____

_____

_____

_____

_____

_____

_____

_____

_____

_____

_____

SUFFERING HAS A PURPOSE

*"Now My soul is troubled. What shall I say? 'Father, save Me
from this hour'? Instead, for this reason I came to this hour.
Father, glorify Your name." Then a voice came from heaven,
saying, "I have glorified it, and will glorify it again."* [1]
—JOHN 12:27–28

WHOSE PURPOSES ARE you serving? It probably seems
as if the answer to that question is, "It appears I'm
just here to please people." And there are so many people to
please. I mean, really, how many people can you please at one
time? It can get maddening. I believe this is what happens to
many Christians who don't understand their purpose in life.
They don't believe strongly in any particular path they are
taking and as a result don't take a stand for anything. If you
don't stand for something, you will fall for everything.

Jesus took a stand for something; He came to set the captives free. He proclaimed it: "The Spirit of the Lord is upon
Me, because He has anointed Me to preach the gospel to the
poor; He has sent Me to heal the broken-hearted, to preach
deliverance to the captives and recovery of sight to the blind,
to set at liberty those who are oppressed" (Luke 4:18). Jesus
gave His life for what He believed in strongly. Jesus knew
that the path the Father had laid out for Him would be one
of suffering. Jesus's love for the Father, His desire to glorify
the Father, and His sense of purpose were the perfect combination for Him to make the ultimate sacrifice.

The sense of significance is a driving force in the human

spirit. It is something many people struggle with their entire lives. They search for love or success and never fully understand that ultimately significance can be found in only one place—the love of the Lord who created them. Throughout history great philosophies and treatises have attempted to answer the question of man's purpose. However, each falls short if it does not have as its centerpiece this one thought: "For this reason I came to this hour. Father, glorify Your name" (John 12:27–28).

HE SUFFERED

Jesus was just like us. He had physical feelings. He shrank from the horror and suffering He must have known were coming. Don't think He didn't have an idea what it meant to be crucified, the pain and humiliation. The nature of self-preservation is that we do not want to suffer. No one makes that choice naturally. It is a challenge for us to understand the redemption that comes from suffering. But it is there, and the benefits are eternal. There are few situations we will encounter that give us the opportunity to cut through the shallowness of life that suffering affords. And perhaps more than anything that can happen to us, suffering brings us closer to the image of Jesus.

Jim and Pam's daughter was just a normal little girl. But as an adult she had a serious drug addiction. It quickly went from bad to disastrous. She lost her job, her home, and her beloved pets. She was in an indescribably desperate place. Counseling, doctors, psychiatrists, psychologists, medications...It was crazy. Jim and Pam couldn't count the number of overdoses. Seizures, emergency medical calls, suicide attempts, being rushed to the hospital time after time—how long could this go on? Their daughter was a depressed, obsessive-compulsive, suicidal drug addict. Then it got worse. She was pregnant. *Impossible.* They committed her to a psychiatric ward more than once. They wondered how long God could keep her alive. They never prayed so much and so long.

Their daughter fell in love and got married. They thought it had gotten even more hopeless because her husband was an illegal alien with no driver's license, no Social Security card, and an expired visa. But it was just the opposite. This guy was absolutely sent by God. He worked three menial jobs, ran the home, watched over the kids, and checked on their daughter every day to see if she was alive. It seemed their prayers were being answered.

An emergency room visit during which the daughter thought she was going to die turned the tide for the parents and daughter. They all confronted the reality—at some point she may die. The parents, through all their prayers, decided to trust the Lord even if she died. Their daughter, as a result of her obsessive disorder, fixated on YouTube gospel videos. She started searching the Scriptures. His Word began to cleanse her life. She stopped abusing drugs and a short time later curtailed the use of all medications. She proclaimed she was healed of the major depression with which she had been diagnosed.

She had been knocking on death's door. Now she is alive. She manages her home, homeschools the children, attends church, and is totally drug free. It is hard to imagine a more complicated, helpless, hopeless situation that had continued for fifteen years. God promises that if we keep knocking, He will answer.

Jim and Pam never wavered in prayer during those fifteen

years of pain and suffering. However, it was during those years that they started leading a large Celebrate Recovery program, which they continue leading today. Celebrate Recovery is a Christ-based approach to recovery that was a response to twelve-step programs such as Alcoholics Anonymous. This couple has deeply touched the lives of hundreds, if not thousands. Their suffering was not wasted, and God was glorified.

REDEMPTION AND RECONCILIATION

Desperation is God's sledgehammer. And nothing throws a person into the throes of desperation like pain and suffering. Desperation shatters strongholds in our lives. For many of us those strongholds are fear and excuses. When desperation takes us beyond our fear and excuses, we begin the process of transformation.

It was foretold that Jesus would be "a man of sorrows" (Isa. 53:3). He was willing to take on sorrows and suffering for our redemption. He was unwavering. Had He chosen a different path, the one apart from suffering, we would have been lost in our sin. His path of suffering reconciled us to God and broke the power of death for eternity. It was His great calling and purpose.

We too have a great calling and purpose. We are to be ministers of reconciliation, His hands in a hurting and dying world. All of us will face monumental sorrows and suffering at some point. Rather than allow it to derail our lives, let us allow suffering to purify and perfect us for the Master's use. If we call upon the Lord during times of suffering, He will use these experiences for our perfection and for His glory. There is a calling and work higher than all others. It does not require advanced degrees or great intellect. It is open to all.

The higher calling is prayer. However, I have discovered that there is a "preparation" for prayer. Few events can prepare us more thoroughly for prayer and being ministers of reconciliation than suffering.

ARE YOU QUALIFIED?

His suffering qualified Him. Let suffering qualify you. In His suffering Christ qualified Himself to break the power of sin and to be our great high priest and intercessor. For we have a great high priest who suffered in every possible way and was victorious. The result: He is able to save us to the uttermost, completely (Heb. 7:25). Let there be no doubt that because of His intercession we can face any temptation, sorrow, or suffering and be victors.

I believe there are two great training grounds where we come to know the Lord intimately. These training grounds prepare us as apprentices to the Master to learn and experience the love of God. Prayer is one of these training grounds; the other is suffering. The school of suffering teaches us dimensions of God's love that can be learned no other way. Through suffering we become more childlike and are poised to bring glory to God. "If we suffer, we shall also reign with him" (2 Tim. 2:12, KJV).

So don't waste your suffering. It has purpose. Allow it to do the work in your life God wants to accomplish. In suffering everything of temporal value is stripped away from our lives, and we discover the majesty and intimacy of Jesus as we cry out to Him in prayer.

When You Pray

Embrace suffering as a training ground in your prayer life.

What is your most painful, ongoing issue in life, whether physical, emotional, relational, or spiritual?

Can you see this suffering as a promotion in your life of faith and an invitation to greater prayer?

_____

_____

_____

_____

_____

_____

_____

_____

_____

_____

_____

_____

_____

DAY 25

MOVING FROM SUBMISSION TO SACRIFICE

"Now My soul is troubled. What shall I say? 'Father, save Me from this hour'? Instead, for this reason I came to this hour. Father, glorify Your name." Then a voice came from heaven, saying, "I have glorified it, and will glorify it again."[1]
—JOHN 12:27–28

HAS YOUR SOUL ever been deeply troubled? It doesn't happen often that a person is distressed to the core of his or her soul. It happens often in the hour of physical pain or affliction, and it can happen during times of great loss. There is even a profound, emotional pain in the core of our being when those closest to us suffer—our children, grandchildren, or spouses. The pain we can suffer reaches such a level that the only response we have is to weep with groanings too deep for words. Our immediate response is to cry out to the Lord to save us from suffering, to deliver us. But the truth is Christians experience cataclysmic events in life like anyone else, from having an illness to being a victim of violence. "Many are the afflictions of the righteous, but the LORD delivers him out of them all" (Ps. 34:19).

Our Lord was not saved from suffering, and even He questioned if He should ask the Father to save Him from that hour. Christ saw the purpose in His suffering—it was to glorify His Father's name. His prayer was answered. He will answer your prayer. We can glorify God through our trials and suffering.

Save Me From This Hour

Anyone who rightly carries spiritual authority knows what it means to be submitted. Every one of us is under authority—many just don't recognize it. I believe there is a spiritual parallel here—the degree that a person is submitted to Christ is the degree to which they are freed and empowered to operate rightly in authority. Whether it is in teaching Sunday school, managing a home, running a business, or doing ministry, the key to authority is submission to the Lord.

Jesus was a man under authority—the Father's. It was the filter through which He made every decision, spoke every word, and did every deed. Correspondingly Jesus spoke with an authority people hadn't heard or seen before. It was the first thing they noticed about Him when He spoke in the synagogue: "They were astonished at His teaching, for His word was with authority" (Luke 4:32).

Jesus gave us an eternal model of what submission should look like. There was no independence in His spirit. He had the full power and knowledge of the universe at His disposal but chose to yield and be human. He submitted. He chose this path because it was the Father's plan. Jesus was the Father's plan to make a way that we might be reconciled to God. Jesus wasn't just partially surrendered in conditions He found expedient. No. He was profoundly given to the Father's plan.

One of the most troubling aspects I encountered in my twenty-plus years of working in Christian organizations is that many Christians couldn't operate under authority, work within the lines of authority, or follow policy. They gossiped about those in leadership and about one another. The spillover effect was predictable—a climate of gossip and division.

Division in a Christian organization happens when people choose not to surrender themselves to Christ and His Word. The Scriptures give us clear direction on how to address conflict, misunderstandings, offenses, and other issues that destroy unity. Some people always seemed to know a better way—theirs.

Jesus was so radically committed to the Father's agenda that He followed it to the cross. The Father's will was Jesus's agenda. As a spiritual leader under submission He set aside personal desires. He expressed His reservations, but in the end He obeyed. "Father, if You are willing, remove this cup from Me. Nevertheless not My will, but Yours, be done" (Luke 22:42).

Jesus took this radical commitment to the Father to a level that challenges us to the deepest realms of our souls. He moved past submission to sacrifice. Serving and sacrificing for others moves far past personal pride and our own plans. Jesus's example of spiritual authority wasn't one of getting to be in charge; it was being the one who served and sacrificed more than anyone.

It's good to slow life down and take a close look at what you are doing. If you have a sense of calling in what you are putting your hands to, then there are some tough questions to ask yourself: Am I serving the purposes of God, or are they serving me? Am I laying my life down? Something deep in my spirit pronounces that if it is not costing me something, it may be illegitimate. I recognize that when Christ beckons a person to follow Him, it is to come and die. If obedience to the Father's plan cost Christ everything, it will cost me something. Jesus said, "If anyone will come after Me, let him deny himself, and take up his cross, and follow Me" (Matt. 16:24).

At some point in our lives each of us faces a friendship, marriage, work relationship, or fellowship (church) experience that is not what we expected. It may be disappointing, boring, seemingly useless, unproductive, or just painful. In those circumstances we have to ask, did God provide this experience? Did He lead me here? If the answer to these questions is yes, then God is at work. He is completing something in our lives. He is working perseverance, commitment, obedience, and other character traits deep into the fabric of our souls.

Everyone has observed people leaving a fellowship of believers disappointed, bored, disillusioned, or hurt because they could not persevere where God had placed them. They become spiritual vagabonds. They wander from church to church. They cannot submit to the Lord. Perhaps you have been one of those people; I know I have at times. But dear reader, please recognize that there is a higher calling. Christ doesn't just call us to submit to His purposes in our lives. He calls us to move from submission to sacrifice, laying down our lives. For it is in this next step that we truly find our life. "For whoever will save his life will lose it, but whoever loses his life for My sake will save it" (Luke 9:24). There is only one way to take this great step of faith—through communion in prayer with the Father in the secret place.

WHEN YOU PRAY

Through prayer the Holy Spirit empowers you to lay down your life for Christ's sake.

Do you have any relationships in your life that are troublesome to your soul?

In light of Christ's prayer in John 12:27–28, write a simple prayer asking the Lord to speak to your heart about these relationships.

Did you sense the Lord directing you to take any specific steps in these relationships?

_____

_____

_____

_____

_____

_____

_____

_____

_____

_____

_____

_____

_____

_____

_____

Day 26

GIVE THANKS

And He took the cup and gave thanks and said, "Take this and divide it among yourselves. For I tell you, I will not drink of the fruit of the vine until the kingdom of God comes." Then He took the bread, and when He had given thanks, He broke it and gave it to them, saying, "This is My body which is given for you. Do this in remembrance of Me." [1]

—LUKE 22:17–19

Jesus gave a simple blessing of thanksgiving, or so it seemed. In blessing (giving thanks) the cup and the bread, Jesus fulfilled the custom of always offering thanks before eating. The thanksgiving was an expression of gratefulness for provision of food. It was one of the items Jesus told us to pray for in what we call the Lord's Prayer: "Give us this day our daily bread" (Matt. 6:11). But this time it represented so much more. The very next day Jesus would open up the kingdom of heaven to everyone through giving His life on the cross.

GRATITUDE

Gratitude is a central part of Christ's prayers, and it is seen time and again in His actions and teachings. Jesus taught us to pray for daily provision and to give thanks for it. It was His practice. We say so many cursory "graces" at mealtimes. Jesus obviously said blessings over meals too, but He spoke in a manner of thanksgiving that was heard in heaven.

Jesus's prayer life is always teaching us. Here, in this

simple thanksgiving at the table, He teaches us to be grateful. We pray for so many things. And rightly so—we should pray about all things: "Be anxious for nothing, but in everything, by prayer and supplication with gratitude, make your requests known to God" (Phil. 4:6). But when our prayers are answered, do we genuinely express thanksgiving? Not a cursory thanks given in haste, but a heartfelt exclamation that resounds to the heart of our Father in heaven? Ingratitude was one of the great failures and sins of the Israelites as they wandered in the desert. They were ungrateful for God's daily provision of manna from heaven. Can you imagine? God provides manna from heaven, and the people grumble all the more.

How different are we from the men in the story Jesus told about the ten lepers? The ten cried out to Jesus for mercy and were healed as they obeyed Him and went and showed themselves to the priests. But only one of them returned to Jesus, giving glory to God with thanksgiving. As you read the story in Luke 17:11–19, it is obvious the focus of the story isn't on the one who returned to give thanks, but on the nine who went on their way. Look at the Lord's somewhat curt response when just one of the ten returns to glorify God his healing: "Were not the ten cleansed? Where are the nine? Were there not any found to return and give glory to God except this foreigner?" (Luke 17:17–18). The focus of the story is to rebuke the ungrateful, not to praise the one grateful leper. It is interesting to note also that Jesus draws attention to the grateful man's ethnicity. He does this to rebuke His followers and any other Jews who did not appreciate that His message of salvation was to the Gentiles also.

Gratefulness Is a Verb

OK, *gratefulness* is a noun, not a verb. However, gratefulness is meaningless unless it leads to action—meaningful action. Living a life of gratefulness will require you to reorient your entire approach to life. It is the supreme paradigm shift, one that requires words to turn to action. The truth is you can often measure a person's gratefulness by the lengths he goes to express it. Sincere, genuine thanks or gratefulness isn't best expressed in a quick text or e-mail. I have received some very kind and thoughtful e-mails, but there are other actions that express a greater depth of gratitude.

Thank You

My handwriting used to be atrocious. My mother-in-law said I wrote in tongues and she had to pray for the interpretation. It was really that bad. Sometimes I couldn't read my own handwritten notes. Many years ago the Lord spoke a clear word to me about gratefulness. The word was simple: express gratefulness, and do it often and in a meaningful way. The primary method I settled on to express gratefulness is the handwritten note. It would be hard to express the positive part that handwritten notes have played in my life. Over a period of two years I taught myself perfect contemporary cursive. When I choose, my handwriting can be flawless. I learned handwriting for one reason. Writing a handwritten note in pristine penmanship is the most personal, classiest way to express thoughts that really matter—in my case thoughts of gratefulness. Don't misunderstand me. Perfect, stylistic handwriting isn't required to write a meaningful thank-you to someone. Yet an ordinary handwritten note is more expressive than the most eloquent of e-mails.

I had been practicing my habit of writing thank-you notes for several years when I began a job at a new school. It was the most negative school I had ever taken over. And I tried every trick I knew to turn it around as the new principal. No success. My personal habit with the thank-you note had worked so well, I thought, "Why not give it a try?" The teachers were mildly resistant at first; however, within just weeks the effects were visible. Student and parent attitudes were changing. What had happened at that school? I required teachers to write one positive note about a student every Friday, and the office mailed the notes home. As the mom of one of the seniors put it, "It was the first time I had ever heard anything positive from the school in four years." It only took one semester for the atmosphere of the school to change dramatically for the good. It was such a simple exercise. But it communicated sincere care to the parents about their students.

HOW FAR WILL YOU GO TO EXPRESS GRATEFULNESS?

When I was in elementary school, I was quite the rascal. My teacher was a wily, bullheaded teacher who didn't give up on anyone. She applied the table tennis paddle to my backside weekly. By the end of the year I had actually made some progress on the road of straight and narrow. There was hope for me. Much to my chagrin, when promotion time to the next grade came, guess who got promoted also? My teacher. Two years with her changed my life. She taught me manners and discipline, and I grew to love her.

When I was a young man having professional success early in life, the Lord spoke to my heart deeply about gratefulness.

He taught me that any degree of success I had experienced was primarily the result of what others had invested in my life. I made a list of those "investors" and contacted each personally. My teacher was at the top of the list. I started by sending her the most heartfelt note I have ever written, and I followed it up with a visit. I drove to the small town in which I had grown up. My teacher, now in her late eighties, lived in a cozy one-bedroom home across from the school where she had spent her lifetime teaching. I was struck by the simplicity and focus of her life. We had a wonderful visit. I heard a few months later that she had passed away one night in her sleep. I wept as I thanked the Lord for the chance to express my gratefulness to her this side of heaven. Oh yes, there is no time like today to express gratefulness.

Prayer and thanksgiving are spiritual partners. "Do not be anxious about anything, but in every situation, by prayer and petition, with thanksgiving, present your requests to God" (Phil. 4:6, NIV). Prayer and thanksgiving empower and enhance each other. Without a thankful spirit the line of communication to God—prayer—is severed. An ungrateful heart can make our prayers less effectual.

The quest to give thanks in all things is challenging, but the Holy Spirit is empowering. By the grace of God we can live our lives in Paul's simple admonition to the Thessalonians: "Rejoice always. Pray without ceasing. In everything give thanks, for this is the will of God in Christ Jesus concerning you" (1 Thess. 5:16–18).

WHEN YOU PRAY

Effective prayer begins with a thankful heart.

Pray and ask the Lord to bring to your remembrance three to five people who contributed the most to any of the different aspects of your life, vocation, spiritual, or personal growth.

Make a plan to express your gratitude to each person over the next few weeks.

_____

_____

_____

_____

_____

_____

_____

_____

_____

_____

_____

_____

_____

_____

GRATEFULNESS IN EVERYTHING?

And He took the cup and gave thanks and said, "Take this and divide it among yourselves. For I tell you, I will not drink of the fruit of the vine until the kingdom of God comes." Then He took the bread, and when He had given thanks, He broke it and gave it to them, saying, "This is My body which is given for you. Do this in remembrance of Me." [1]
—LUKE 22:17–19

LIFE PASSES BY quickly. I often hear the phrase "Slow things down, and enjoy the moment." That is one of the real challenges of life because our pace is so frantic. We need to quit looking to the next thing and appreciate the sweet nuances of the moment. OK, that seems easy. We can work on that. But what about the moments that are not so sweet?

GRATITUDE IN THE FACE OF SUFFERING

Have you experienced suffering? Have you been in the place where you can't wait for something to end because it is so hard, painful, humiliating, or downright depressing? How many times have you said to yourself, "I can't wait to get through this," or, "Surely this is going to end soon"? It seems like such foolishness to consider slowing down in these kinds of moments to appreciate them before they pass. But that is the difference between the wisdom of man and the wisdom of God. "For the foolishness of God is wiser than men, and the weakness of God is stronger than men" (1 Cor. 1:25).

Jesus was on the cusp of the most violent, disgusting, and humiliating death a human could face—crucifixion. He knew what the cup represented. He knew what the breaking of the bread represented. Yet He gave thanks for them. Was He just giving thanks because it was part of the Passover tradition, or was He giving thanks because He was able to see beyond the suffering to the redemption it would bring?

Jesus knew completely the impending suffering and sacrifice to come but gave thanks that His blood was about to be poured out and His body broken. Many of us have the grit to just endure when we find ourselves in the throes of some harrowing predicament. We marshal all our resources and suffer through the best we can. However, crucifixion is altogether different and on a higher plain of misery. In the face of the prospect of this monumental suffering and sacrifice, Jesus gave thanks.

Giving thanks in the face of suffering seems altogether farfetched. Who could take us seriously? However, this is precisely what God beckons us to do. It's the instruction Paul gave to his young disciple Timothy: "Rejoice always. Pray without ceasing. In everything give thanks, for this is the will of God in Christ Jesus concerning you" (1 Thess. 5:16–18). It can absolutely be the same experience for us. If we give ourselves to God and allow the Holy Spirit to work through us, God will help us do the impossible. He will enable us to give thanks in the midst of profound suffering and sacrifice, knowing that His plans for us are good and He is working all things together for our good (Jer. 29:11; Rom. 8:28).

SELF-PITY

The problem with suffering and sacrifice is the responses that come so naturally to us. Ingratitude seems to be fully justified in the face of intense pain or suffering. Yet this ingratitude usually lands on those who are doing the most for us, those closest to us. There are so many other feelings we easily submit to, such as depression, rebellion, and the most wasteful emotion of all—self-pity.

Self-pity is a deceptive sin. It is natural (so we tell ourselves) to have outrage at what we are going through. Feelings of anger come so easily. Somehow we feel vindicated in wallowing in our disgust, considering what we are suffering. We tell ourselves we don't deserve this. In its deceit self-pity opens the door to all types of ungodly retreats: substance abuse, pornography, or bingeing on whatever will take our minds off of our suffering. Every relationship we have eventually will be poisoned by self-pity.

Dealing with self-pity requires intense honesty with yourself. As an individual you have to stomp on the head of self-pity and repent. No one else can do this for you. However, addressing self-pity also means seeking the help of others. As much as self-pity is on your shoulders to harness, the quickest way out of it is confessing the sin to someone close in your life. That will be a huge blow to pride—just what the Lord ordered.

When we give in to these emotional indulgences that come from catastrophic events—such as seeking healing and not finding it, losing a loved one, finding out a spouse is cheating, or going through a bout of cancer—we short-circuit God. He intends for all these experiences to drive us into a deeper dimension of trust, faith, and character development, but prayer is the key—our own prayers and the prayers of others. There is no greater gift others can give us, but it requires a humble submission to their petitions to reap the full benefit of prayer. Prayer gives us listening ears to what God is saying.

During my years of pain and suffering I started asking the Lord, "What?," instead of, "Why?" "Why?" is the question of a victim. "What?" is the question of a warrior, an over-comer. I eventually asked the Lord, "What are You doing in my life? What do You want to accomplish?" His answer was simple and somehow reassuring. He wanted me to submit all of my life to Him. On the other hand, though, His answer seemed puzzling. I lost my job, was losing my house, was out of the limelight, and was relegated to a chair most of the time. There seemed little left to submit. But the Lord had my full attention. He then spoke something to my heart that was deep and, honestly, rather offensive: Can you give Me the last reservoir of yourself? Can you give Me every word that comes out of your mouth? Can you fill your mouth with praise and thanksgiving instead of complaining?

I set out on this quest and spent months allowing the Holy Spirit to excavate the swampland and deep reservoirs of my soul and heart. Just when I thought every word in my mouth was submitted, the Holy Spirit went for the gold.

The Holy Spirit asked for even my sounds. In my pain I groaned, moaned, ached, and made an assortment of sounds. I thought to myself, "Surely I have the right to moan; I am in intense pain." The Spirit invited me to listen to myself for a few days. The discovery was like a brilliant light shining on my heart. In the depths of my heart I was still reaching out in self-pity. Someone had to understand my pain. Listening to myself a little longer and deeper, I discovered my painful sounds were emitted less when I was alone and more when I was around my wife, the one who cared for me, prayed for me, and stood by my side through good times and not so good times. Honestly I am still reaching out for complete victory in this last bastion of submission. But prayer broke the cycle of distress I was in emotionally, deep in my soul; now my heart is tender, and I am moving up higher with the Lord constantly.

By the power of the Holy Spirit we can give thanks in any situation. There is no mountain in life that we cannot climb with great joy. Whether it is great suffering, discipline, or opportunities for character development, the Holy Spirit is our helper. We are not left to our own devices. Our heavenly Father is at work. He is taking us to a place of complete surrender where we will experience the fullness of all He has for us and give thanks in everything.

When You Pray

Christ desires joy and thanksgiving in all circumstances to be a divine reality in your life.

Is there a place in your life where you quickly fall into self-pity? Does it open the door for sinful habits? Seek the Lord for forgiveness today.

Ask the Lord to help you be thankful despite any trying circumstances you are facing.

_____

_____

_____

_____

_____

THE INTERCESSOR

Then the Lord said, "Simon, Simon, listen! Satan has demanded to have
you to sift you as wheat. But I have prayed for you that your faith may
not fail. And when you have repented, strengthen your brothers." [1]
—LUKE 22:31–32

CONFUSION WAS EVERYWHERE. Jesus had told the
disciples He must suffer, and it became clear that He
was going to die. Emotions were running high. As if it
couldn't get worse, Christ proceeded to tell them that one
of them would betray Him. Betray Him? How could this
be? They had experienced so much together. Yet in a matter
of moments the disciples went from trying to identify the
betrayer to arguing about which one of them would be
regarded as greatest.

It is no coincidence that Jesus's short time of ministry
brought Him into direct confrontation with the religious and
political powers of the day, so much so that His life was in
danger. Through His actions in the temple Jesus challenged
the chief priests, who made convenient arrangements with
the Romans, and He did it in a manner that no one ever had
or would have dared. His confrontation with the Pharisees
could not have been more volatile and embarrassing to this
sociopolitical group of Jews obsessed with man-made rules.
The disciples knew Jesus's life was in danger. But to say that
one of them would betray Him was just too much. Could it
have gotten any more troubling to them? Yes. Satan entered

the scene, demanding to sift Peter like wheat to see if his faith would fail.

I Have Prayed for You

In Luke 22:31 Jesus spoke to Peter as if His interaction with Satan had already taken place. It is a scene reminiscent of Satan's attack on Job. Jesus knew the hour was coming quickly when Peter would deny Him three times. Because Jesus had interceded for Peter, He knew and proclaimed what would take place in the near future. Jesus pronounced the outcome of His intercession for Peter: "And when you have repented, strengthen your brothers" (Luke 22:32). Did you grasp that? Jesus knew trials were coming. He knew what Peter would be facing. He knew that during one of the most difficult times of His life on earth, one of His closest friends would deny Him. Yet He interceded for Peter. He interceded knowing that Peter would hurt Him. And because of His intercession, He knew what the end result would be for Peter. Amazing love!

Jesus Christ intercedes for us just as He did for Peter. He knows the trials we are facing. He knows we are going to do things that hurt Him. Yet He still intercedes for us. His plan has always been to restore us, just as Peter was restored after his denial of Christ. (See John 21.) In His high priestly prayer Jesus prayed for the disciples and everyone who would follow Him. As intimately as Jesus interceded for Peter, He intercedes for us now. The work of Christ's intercession is never-ending.

What Is an Intercessor?

Most people regard intercession as just a form of deeper or more intense prayer. But what makes intercession different from everyday prayer is altogether so much more.

An intercessor is one who gives himself to God in prayer to bring down the power of God on earth, one who is alert and sensitive to the leading of the Holy Spirit. An intercessor devotes himself to prayer for others and answers the call for persistence and perseverance in prayer for requests such as this one Paul expressed in Colossians: "Devote yourselves to prayer, keeping alert in it with an attitude of thanksgiving; praying at the same time for us as well, that God will open up to us a door for the word, so that we may speak forth the mystery of Christ, for which I have also been imprisoned (Col. 4:2–3, NASB).

An intercessor carves out the time to present himself before God and listen. He has learned not to pray for selfish needs but instead has had his heart enlarged. We simply do not see blessings to others in prayer as we should because selfishness stifles prayer. Becoming an intercessor takes you to a place where you are genuinely more concerned for others than yourself.

CHRIST THE INTERCESSOR

In Christ we see the perfect example of an intercessor: "Therefore I will divide Him a portion with the great, and He shall divide the spoil with the strong, because He poured out His soul unto death, and He was numbered with the transgressors, and He bore the sin of many, and made intercession for the transgressors" (Isa. 53:12, NKJV).

Christ attained the position of intercessor with complete authority to call down God's power. In His intercession He gave His life for those for whom He pleaded. He plunged Himself into their needs with great urgency and took their place. He had no self-interest. Christ crucified the flesh.

Intercession is one of Christ's greatest works on earth. Christ came in human form so that He might intercede for us. And as Christ left this world, He gave this work of intercession to us: "You did not choose Me, but I chose you, and appointed you, that you should go and bear fruit, and that your fruit should remain, that the Father may give you whatever you ask Him in My name" (John 15:16). Christ's kingdom is established in our midst by the intercession of the saints. Even now, as He is seated at the right hand of the Father, He continues to be our High Priest, interceding for us. He battles in heaven for our completion, perfection, and fullness of faith. "Therefore He is able to save to the uttermost those who come to God through Him, because He at all times lives to make intercession for them" (Heb. 7:25).

THE FATHER ALWAYS SEEKS INTERCESSORS

God seeks intercessors but rarely finds them. The Almighty exclaimed through Isaiah "that there was no man and [He] was astonished that there was no intercessor; therefore, His own arm brought salvation to Him, and His righteousness sustained Him" (Isa. 59:16). He expressed His regret through Ezekiel: "I sought for a man among them who would build up the hedge and stand in the gap before Me for the land so that I would not destroy it, but I found no one" (Ezek. 22:30).

Still, the Word of God provides manifest examples of those who sacrificed their lives to find that place of intercession, men and women whom God called to reject all natural reason, crucify their flesh, and follow Him in intercession. These examples are as astounding as they are inspiring and scandalous to our carnal thinking.

+ Moses—He interceded for the Israelites following their blasphemy and idolatry in worshipping a golden calf. The Lord was so angry with Aaron and the people that He wanted to destroy them. However, after Moses fasted for forty days and nights, the Lord spared them. "I fell down before the LORD, as at the first, forty days and forty nights. I did not eat bread or drink water because of all your sins which you committed, doing what was wicked in the sight of the LORD to provoke Him to anger. For I was afraid of the anger and hot displeasure with which the LORD was wrathful against you to destroy you. But the LORD listened to me at that time also" (Deut. 9:18–19).

+ Isaiah—"The LORD said, 'Even as My servant Isaiah has walked naked and barefoot three years for a sign and wonder against Egypt and Ethiopia….'" (Isa. 20:3). Who could believe such a thing—a recognized prophet dressing so scandalously (in only his undergarments) that compared with others he might be said to go naked? Can you imagine the contempt and ridicule he would encounter? I am sure many wrote him off as a fool or madman. Nonetheless, God had Isaiah do it to show his obedience and to shame the disobedience of His people. The people's hearts were hardened to what they heard, so Isaiah was called upon by God to intercede and be a visible sign. He was to signify that the Egyptians and Ethiopians would be led away into captivity by the king of Assyria, stripped of their fine clothes.

+ Hosea—"Then the Lord said to me, 'Go, again, love a woman who is loved by a lover and is committing adultery, just as the Lord loves the children of Israel, who look to other gods and love raisin cakes'" (Hosea 3:1). Hosea was directed by God to stay married to an adulterous wife in order to intercede and show the Israelites a living picture of their relationship with Him. Though the Israelites were repeatedly unfaithful, they were chosen of God and yet loved by Him. God promised to redeem them and always love them because they were His covenant people.

+ Paul—Over many years Paul offered himself as a living sacrifice in order to bring the gospel to the Gentiles. Hear the depth of his intercession for his kinsmen, the people of Israel, as he states that he would subject himself to being cut off from the church if it would bring the Jews to Christ. "For I could wish that I myself were accursed from Christ for my brothers, my kinsmen by race, who are Israelites, to whom belong the adoption, the glory, the covenants, the giving of the law, the service of God, and the promises" (Rom. 9:3–4).

There have been many other intercessors who stood in the gap for their generations and found a place of abiding in God to move God and even cause Him to change His mind. Their sacrifices are inspiring, and their intercession was world changing.

+ William Booth—He interceded for the poorest and neediest, including alcoholics, criminals, and prostitutes. Despite being castigated by church leaders,

Booth brought the message of hope through Christ to the hopeless around the globe.[2]

+ Hudson Taylor—He interceded for China, founding the China Inland Mission in the nineteenth century, which led to thousands of conversions and hundreds of missionaries giving their lives for China.[3]

+ Dietrich Bonhoeffer—He stood in the gap for Germany during one of the darkest times in history. He left the safe confines of America to return to his homeland and fearlessly resist Hitler. He was vocal in his opposition to Hitler's euthanasia program and genocidal persecution of the Jews while discipling and encouraging many in the underground church. His martyrdom was predictable.[4]

+ Mother Teresa—She was the intercessor for India. She founded the Order of the Missionaries of Charity, which today is active in 123 countries. The members of the order run hospices and homes for those with leprosy and HIV/AIDS, dispensaries and mobile clinics, orphanages, schools, and many more out-reaches to the poorest of the poor.[5]

Don't be overwhelmed at the magnificence of interces-sors listed here. The pages of this book could be filled with individuals and small groups that are directly responsible for ushering in some of the greatest revivals in history. When it comes to intercession, one is always a majority with God. He is calling you today to be one of the many ones.

WHEN YOU PRAY

God has called you to be an intercessor.

Wait on the Lord today in prayer. Ask Him for a specific assignment of intercession He has reserved for you. Write down your assignment, and begin today to be the intercessor God has called you to be.

Chronicle in your journal the ways you intercede, and watch for the Lord's answer to your intercession. Answers are on the way.

_____

_____

_____

_____

_____

_____

_____

_____

_____

_____

_____

_____

_____

Day 29

THE POWER OF INTERCESSION

Then the Lord said, "Simon, Simon, listen! Satan has demanded to have you to sift you as wheat. But I have prayed for you that your faith may not fail. And when you have repented, strengthen your brothers." [1]
—LUKE 22:31–32

T HIS POWER OF the Holy Spirit in intercession is not something for just a select few. Let this marinate deep in your soul: you are not disqualified from or inadequate for interceding for others. The same Holy Spirit that enables men and women to stand in the gap for nations, people, groups, and individuals is standing at the doorstep of your heart today. The Lord makes the spirit of prayer and intercession available for all who desire to be filled with His Spirit. It is the power of intercession that will see the prayer of Christ fulfilled: "Your kingdom come; Your will be done on earth, as it is in heaven" (Matt. 6:10).

THE INVITATION IS OPEN

The invitation is open for you to become an intercessor. Intercession can be as simple as standing in the gap for one person. Don't let the thought of becoming more concerned for someone else than yourself keep you from crying out for this spirit of intercession. Yes, there is a cost, and it is a divine reality, not some ethereal, unseen sacrifice. But be assured, the Holy Spirit will direct your life in this.

Are you willing to accept the invitation? Are you willing

to pour yourself out for the sake of another and for the sake of His kingdom?

TWO PERSONAL EXAMPLES

Please read these in the spirit with which they are written: brokenness and humility. I am a regular person, flawed by my upbringing, worldliness, and sin. I have intimacy issues. I am still "in the process" of expanding my faith and possibilities for intercession. I could go on. But none of my failures are greater than the Lord's forgiveness and redemption.

Several years ago I was drawn to pray for a young woman I had never met. She previously had respiratory issues, had contracted pneumonia in both lungs, and was in the ICU. Over the course of the next few days her situation became life-threatening. I don't understand why, but the Holy Spirit began to weigh heavily on me with a burden for intercession for someone I had never met and probably never would. It was one of the first occasions I felt this invitation to intercession and answered it.

The situation worsened to the point that the girl was critical and not expected to live. The immediate family was called to be with her in the ICU. I had some time off from work and was in the process of doing some work in a house where it was quiet and I was by myself. I decided to hunker down in prayer. I remember asking the Lord, "What do You want to do?" Out of the abyss this thought came to me: "Cry out to Me ten thousand times for her, and I will glorify Myself through her." My immediate thought was that I was conjuring that up or having a hallucination. I put pen to paper and calculated how many times per minute I could cry out to the Lord, "Lord, heal [the young woman]," and I could reach ten thousand in approximately eleven hours. I had the time, and I thought I had the gall and the faith. After approximately seventy-five hundred cries out to the Lord I was worn out, had no more tears, and had no voice. Feeling defeated, I stopped and waited patiently on the Lord to speak. As clearly as you have probably had the Lord speak to you on occasions through His Word, dreams, or other ways, the Lord said to me, "This isn't about you. I just needed someone to stand in the gap."

I heard that the young woman made an almost immediate turnaround and in a matter of days was out of the hospital, completely healed.

Another time one of the marvelous women of prayer in our church was fighting for her life with stage IV cancer. Many were praying and interceding. She and her husband had been rejected for treatment at one of the major cancer facilities in the United States. Her oncologist had told her she was too advanced for further treatment. She was withering in pain, and they didn't know where to turn.

A particular morning I had blocked out about three hours to pray, read, study, and meditate on the Word. My wife was out of the country on a mission trip, so I had time to myself and wanted to spend it in my favorite pursuit—intimacy with Jesus. I even got up early that morning to start, and I had no sooner begun than the Spirit of the Lord whispered to my heart, "Lay everything aside, and pray for this woman." Honestly, I fought the thought, skirted around it, and stalled for almost an hour before I gave in, set everything aside, and interceded for a few hours for her. It was only a matter of days before inexplicably and miraculously the woman was contacted by the facility that had rejected her. She was accepted as a patient and started on a rigorous course of treatment, which put her cancer into remission.

QUALITIES OF AN INTERCESSOR

The most outstanding quality of an intercessor is seeing the need at hand as more important than your own need. It is a severe challenge to be identified with someone to the point that the other person's need outweighs yours. This is the beginning place of intercession—identifying with the one you are interceding for, being his or her authentic representative, crucifying the self, and becoming consumed by the other's need.

The possibilities of intercession develop as a person allows the Lord to touch everything in him that loves the world. Affections, appetites, the love of money, even reputation—the Holy Spirit leaves no stone unturned as He prepares the heart for intercession. It is no happenstance that in Jesus's final discourse in John 14–16 He made the disciples clearly aware of the rift between Him and the world and them and the world. Jesus even went as far as to say the world would not recognize the Helper that He was sending the disciples: "He will give you another Helper, that He may abide with you forever—the Spirit of truth, whom the world cannot receive, because it neither sees Him nor knows Him; but you know Him, for He dwells with you and will be in you" (John 14:16–17, NKJV).

Another important characteristic of intercession is authority. The workings of the Holy Spirit in a person, identifying with others, and being crucified to the world all lead to one place: authority in prayer. The source of the power and authority in prayer comes from abiding in the vine

(John 15:1–8). We are crucified with Christ and now live by faith (Gal. 2:20). There is a place of intercession that can be gained in the spirit where the Word of the Lord will come and the Holy Spirit will teach us how and what to pray. Our thoughts and prayers come into agreement with Him.

STRENGTHEN THE BROTHERS

It is difficult for us to grasp within our "Christian" culture in the United States that if we follow Christ, it is going to bring us into conflict. The time is near, or perhaps even here, when there may be a tangible cost to the Christian who follows Christ wholeheartedly and biblically. The days of the cultural popularity of true Christianity in the United States are waning. There are many topics up for discussion today that have a great polarizing effect. Simply trying to live a biblical lifestyle on any of a number of these issues may lead to your being ostracized, criticized, or even penalized by others in concrete ways. Your life and obedience to Christ will be a living rebuke to half-hearted, lukewarm Christianity.

"Strengthen your brothers" (Luke 22:32). That is what Jesus saw as Peter's role in the future after he repented. Who among us has not had failures in the quest to follow the Lord? It is not the size of our failure that matters; it is the greatness of Christ's forgiveness that makes the difference. It is His forgiveness that woos us back to following Him and continuing to grow in the grace and knowledge of Christ, growing to the place where we can strengthen others. When Christ has brought you to a place of repentance, be willing to use what you have learned to strengthen others—encourage, exhort, and most of all, intercede.

When I was a young man, I met with a group of other

young men in a discipleship setting. We wondered and spoke aloud, "Where are the older, gray-haired men who would show us the way, impart the life of God to us, and invest in our lives?" Now I know where they are. I have seen godly man after godly man fall away or never be able to grab hold of this magnificent truth: Christ will forgive a man and restore him. Christ has called each of us as he called Peter to "strengthen [our] brothers." Paul later echoed these thoughts when he told young Timothy, "Share the things that you have heard from me in the presence of many witnesses with faithful men who will be able to teach others also" (2 Tim. 2:2). Paul also specifically exhorted the women: "Likewise, older women should be reverent in behavior, and not be false accusers, not be enslaved to much wine, but teachers of good things, that they may teach the young women to love their husbands, to love their children, and to be self-controlled, pure, home-makers, good, obedient to their own husbands, that the word of God may not be dishonored" (Titus 2:3–5). Translation: strengthen your sisters. Whether you are a man or a woman, this is what Jesus sees in the future for you. Through intercession you can strengthen your brothers and sisters in the body of Christ.

As Christ prayed for us, He wants us to learn to pray and intercede for others. Is it a daunting task? Absolutely. However, this is the will of God in Christ Jesus. And Christ Himself is interceding for us (Rom. 8:34; Heb 7:25) along with the Holy Spirit. "Likewise, the Spirit helps us in our weaknesses, for we do not know what to pray for as we ought, but the Spirit Himself intercedes for us with groanings too deep for words. He who searches the hearts knows what the mind of the Spirit is, because He intercedes for the saints according to the will of God" (Rom. 8:26–27).

WHEN YOU PRAY

There is dynamic power in the Holy Spirit that will strengthen you and others through intercession. Will you answer the call?

In humble and honest reflection, ask the Lord these questions today: Is there a particular area of my life that is not submitted to You? Is there an area that is holding me back from considering another person's needs?

_____

_____

_____

_____

_____

_____

_____

_____

_____

_____

_____

_____

DAY 30

JESUS'S MISSION STATEMENT

Holy Father, through Your name keep those whom You have given Me, that they may be one as We are one.... I say these things in the world, that they may have My joy fulfilled in themselves.... I do not pray that You should take them out of the world, but that You should keep them from the evil one.... Sanctify them by Your truth. Your word is truth.... I do not pray for these alone, but also for those who will believe in Me through their word, that they may all be one, as You, Father, are in Me, and I in You. May they also be one in Us, that the world may believe that You have sent Me ... that they may be perfect in unity, and that the world may know that You have sent Me, and have loved them as You have loved Me.... I have declared Your name to them, and will declare it, that the love with which You loved Me may be in them, and I in them.
—JOHN 17:11, 13, 15, 17, 20–21, 23, 26

PICTURE THE SCENE in your mind's eye. There is no more time for parables, healings, or miracles; the hour has come. It's here. In a short period of time Jesus will cross the ravine of Kidron to the garden where Judas will betray Him. He is speaking His last words to the disciples before the crucifixion. What's He going to say? What is the most critical message with which to leave them?

He begins a conversation with God and prays to the Father in their presence. It is so typical of Jesus, almost predictable—He prays. Jesus prays for the disciples, that they would be one with one another as He is one with the Father. He prays that they might be protected from the evil one, that they will be sanctified, that they would have His joy, and that all who believe in Him will experience these benefits.

JESUS'S VISION STATEMENT

If there were ever an executive vision or mission statement, this is it, the High Priestly Prayer. The longest recorded prayer of Jesus is a prayer that transcends time. It reveals Jesus's intention for all who would commit their lives to Him—that they will become one with the Father, with Him, and with one another. It makes known Jesus's plan to convince the world He was sent from God. How? By the complete unity of His followers. And this prayer discloses the eternal outcome for all those who give themselves to Him—that they will be with Him in glory.

UNITY

We obviously undervalue unity and the power of believers praying in unity. Unity was Jesus's plan. It was His strategy to reach the lost. It was His plan to convince the world that He was the Son of God. He didn't have a backup proposal or a plan B. It was all or nothing. John 17:21 says, "…that they may all be one, as You, Father, are in Me, and I in You. May they also be one in Us, that the world may believe that You have sent Me." The plan was simple—we show to others the love that was in God toward Christ and that Christ showed to us, and the world will be overwhelmed with the authenticity of Christianity.

Christians Who Care

One of my employees in a Christian school was a single mom with two adopted children. Single mom, one income, private school, high school-age daughter—you can image the strain on the budget. She had just moved from an apartment to a house. The house was a fixer-upper, but it ended up being a disaster. Roof, electric, plumbing, drywall, floors, you name it—it had to be replaced, remodeled, and modernized. She spent everything she could afford and was left with an unfinished, unfurnished house. The mom went off for a week to a conference, and while she was gone, parents descended on her home. They finished the trim throughout the house, installed doors, put down rugs, hung curtains and blinds, hung pictures and artwork throughout the house, and brought in beautiful bedroom furniture, couches, and chairs. They organized belongings and finished the garage. All in all, thousands of dollars worth of brand-new furnishings was donated. This kind of care and love for one another has become a hallmark of the community surrounding this Christian school. Oh, how they care for one another.

My wife and I are friends with a husband and wife who are the most generous Christian people we have ever known. These two set the standard for generosity, and their generosity began long before they were wealthy. While he was in his early thirties, the husband was mowing lawns for a living with six children and a wife to support. He decided to change occupations, went back to school, and became an optometrist. Today he and his wife are wealthy by man's standards. But it is God who has blessed his businesses. You would never know of their wealth because of their lifestyle. They give to others scandalously.

One of many examples of their generosity was when a missionary couple came home for a short furlough. Our friends gave the missionaries their entire house for a month. Our friends moved out of their house! They gave the missionaries one of their best cars to drive. The missionary couple was invited to have the whole family (five grown children) come home for the holidays at the house. Wow! Oh, how Christians can care for one another. John 17:23: "…that they may be perfect in unity, and that the world may know that You have sent Me."

LOVE ONE ANOTHER

Everything was stacked against the survival of the early church. They were a small, hated group. They were up against the powerful Roman Empire. The early church experienced persecution after persecution that was meant to extinguish it completely. So how did this fledgling movement survive, thrive, and eventually outlast the great Roman Empire? The answer is simple: they loved one another in unity.

Amazingly the Christians of the early church actually displayed the love of God toward Christ among one another and toward the people of the time—the Romans, Jews, and Greeks. The people the Christians lived with had a great animosity toward everyone except those who were among their numbers. The love that the Christians had toward those outside of their group was a completely unknown concept. Nonetheless, all these groups witnessed the Christians loving one another and even them. Their love could not be denied. Emperor Julian, who was an enemy of Christianity, stated, "The godless Galileans care not only for their own poor but for ours as well."[1] Tertullian penned that the Christians' love was so authentic that the pagans voiced in surprise, "See how they love one another."[2]

It is no wonder Christianity spread like wildfire. Unity worked. It worked because the disciples experienced the fullness of life in the Spirit. The disciples experienced the power of unified prayer. They proved that Jesus's promise was true. In those ten days before Pentecost they prayed continually in unity. They received the power of the Holy Spirit and turned around and imparted it to thousands. This promise is no less true for us today. If we patiently wait and are united with others in prayer, we can receive the power of the Holy Spirit to change the lives of others. People will see and believe that Jesus is the Son of God.

WHEN YOU PRAY

Unity with other believers reveals the reality of Christ.

Are there particular Christians with whom you find it challenging to walk in unity?

Ask the Lord today to guide you and reveal tangible steps you can take toward unity with these specific people.

_____

_____

_____

_____

_____

_____

ENGAGING THE ENEMY
IN SPIRITUAL WARFARE

*Holy Father, through Your name keep those whom You have given
Me, that they may be one as We are one.... I say these things in
the world, that they may have My joy fulfilled in themselves.... I
do not pray that You should take them out of the world, but that
You should keep them from the evil one.... Sanctify them by Your
truth. Your word is truth.... I do not pray for these alone, but
also for those who will believe in Me through their word, that they
may all be one, as You, Father, are in Me, and I in You. May they
also be one in Us, that the world may believe that You have sent
Me... that they may be perfect in unity, and that the world may
know that You have sent Me, and have loved them as You have loved
Me.... I have declared Your name to them, and will declare it, that
the love with which You loved Me may be in them, and I in them.*
—JOHN 17:11, 13, 15, 17, 20–21, 23, 26

WE NEED TO learn this lesson—we experience the Lord
three ways: through our personal experience, through
the Word and prayer, and through our fellowship with
others in our community. In all three of these realms Satan
is at war to destroy God's essential purpose. He attacks the
intimacy we find in Christ through our personal experiences.
Our personal experiences with Christ are the basis from
which all spiritual life flows. The enemy constantly attacks
the credibility of God's Word and diverts our attention
away from prayer. Satan does this because he knows it is

through the Word and prayer that we mature as Christians and become equipped to battle against him. And the enemy schemes to create division in our fellowship with other believers because he understands that division will discredit the love of Christ. Disunity in the body of Christ will cause people to doubt if Jesus really is who He said He is, the Son of God. The consequence of this disunity in the body is devastating to the spread of the gospel. Much of Jesus's prayer in John 17 addresses His plea to the Father for the unity of believers with Them (the Father and Son) and with one another (vv. 11, 21–23).

Spiritual Warfare

The Word of God reveals that there is a furious spiritual battle taking place right now in the heavens and the unseen realms (Eph. 6:12). Most of us are unaware of this war. If we have an awareness of spiritual warfare from the Scriptures, we don't really believe in it or that we have been called to participate. There is an additional rebutting that takes place with many Christians when it comes to spiritual warfare: it is a disturbing concept for us. The thought of battling demons, evil spirits, or Satan himself is overwhelming and frightening. But here is the truth of the gospel: much of the world has come under the influence of Satan, as he rules the world. "The god of this world has blinded the minds of those who do not believe, lest the light of the glorious gospel of Christ, who is the image of God, should shine on them" (2 Cor. 4:4).

Just because we have accepted Christ and go to church does not mean we are immune from the attacks and influence of Satan. When we choose to walk in darkness and sin and not respond to Christ, we open ourselves up to the enemy.

We are warned by Christ to be cautious and be sure we are walking in the light, not darkness. "The eye is the lamp of the body. Therefore when your eye is good, your whole body also is full of light. But when your eye is bad, your body also is full of darkness. Take heed therefore lest the light which is in you is darkness" (Luke 11:34–35).

WHERE'S THE BATTLE?

Satan dwells in the darkness. This is where he and all his demons (fallen angels) were sent to by God (Luke 10:18; 2 Pet. 2:4; Jude 6; Rev. 12:4). Where is the darkness? We need to understand that any place the knowledge of God is absent is darkness, and darkness is the domain of the enemy. The most intense part of the battle is here.

Where Christ is, there is light and the darkness is dispelled. Jesus said, "I am the light of the world. Whoever follows Me shall not walk in the darkness, but shall have the light of life" (John 8:12). People who do not follow Jesus walk in darkness. Before you came to know the Lord as your Savior, you were in the kingdom of darkness. You lived in this world physically, but you lived in Satan's territory spiritually. The moment you accepted Jesus as your Savior, you were transported into God's kingdom. It makes no difference now where you live physically, whether or not you live under persecution, or if you are affluent or impoverished—if Christ is your Savior, you live in His kingdom. "For He rescued us from the domain of darkness, and transferred us to the kingdom of His beloved Son" (Col. 1:13, NASB).

The battle is furious in the unseen realm. This is why our weapons in spiritual warfare are not carnal or fleshly. The enemy wars against us as we pursue God to have His kingdom established in our minds, emotions, and wills (our souls). The enemy is actively planning schemes, diversions, rear attacks, and every other evil plan to cast doubt in the minds of men and women concerning God's Word. The enemy entices our emotions and wills to be captured by the world—"the lust of the flesh," "the lust of the eyes," and "the...pride of life" (1 John 2:16). So many Christians find themselves trapped in sexual addictions, pornography, and other types of perversions and compulsive behaviors, never realizing that they are losing a spiritual battle. They try to fight the battle with worldly weapons that yield little success. They haven't been taught to wage war in the unseen and heavenly realm.

We Are All Called to the Battle

Make no mistake—every Christian is called to spiritual warfare. The enemy is seeking to destroy us (1 Pet. 5:8). Our spiritual survival depends upon being able to discern the enemy; repel his attacks, temptations, and schemes; and stand against the powers of darkness. God has called every one of us into His spiritual army (2 Tim. 2:3–4).

God has not called us to just stand and defend ourselves in battle. He has called us to use the weapons of our warfare to defeat the enemy and crush him underfoot (Rom. 8:37–39; 16:20; 1 John 2:13–14). Everyday people such as you and me are called to put on the armor of light and cast aside the works of darkness (Rom. 13:12). We are called to bring God's kingdom of heaven to earth: "Your kingdom come; Your will be done on earth, as it is in heaven" (Matt. 6:10).

WAGING WAR

The primary weapons God puts at our disposal are the sword of the Spirit (the Word of God) and Spirit-empowered prayer. Along with the weapons, He equips us with an armor that the enemy cannot penetrate. Arrayed in this armor, we can withstand any onslaught Satan throws at us. (Please read and study Ephesians 6:10–20.) But we must put on the armor. If you enter warfare with the enemy and are not completely surrendered to Christ in every area of your life, you will be defeated or wounded at best. So put on your armor—all of it. Paul exhorts us, "Put on the whole armor of God that you may be able to stand against the schemes of the devil" (Eph. 6:11). So put on the belt of truth, the breastplate of righteousness, the shoes of the gospel of peace, and the helmet of salvation, and take up the shield of faith and the sword of the Spirit (Eph. 6:14–17). Put on the whole armor of God, and take a stand to resist the devil.

Worship is another powerful weapon that God puts at our disposal. Our worship can take many forms—singing, dancing, praying, playing instruments, or raising our hands. Worship will build up our faith in God and keep our focus on Him, the source of our strength to battle (1 Sam. 17:47; Rom. 4:20–21). There are numerous examples in Scripture in which worship won the battle (Judg. 7:15; 2 Chron. 20:22; Acts 16:25–26).

Through prayer and the Word of God we are able to discern the strongholds of the enemy and tear down his defenses (2 Cor. 10:4–5). Practically this means we can bring thoughts and speculations in our own lives under the control of the Spirit. We will demolish fears that have held us in check: the fear of failure, the fear of man, the fear of the future, and so many other strongholds. "For God has not given us the spirit of fear, but of power, and love, and self-control" (2 Tim. 1:7). We will be freed from chains of the past that have caused us to live the past in the present every day. We will no longer be prisoners of the past. "For freedom Christ freed us. Stand fast therefore and do not be entangled again with the yoke of bondage" (Gal. 5:1). The powers of darkness may rule in the unseen, but the powers of darkness will be broken in our lives and the lives of others as we learn to war in the spirit. We will be God's warriors, fully equipped to see the forces of evil destroyed and His kingdom established in our midst.

When You Pray

Through prayer God wants us to learn to discern the enemy's schemes and destroy his strongholds in our lives.

As you seek the Lord today in quietness and stillness, do you sense any calling to spiritual warfare?

Is the Lord speaking to you about any of your own spiritual battlegrounds? If so, list some of them, and ask the Lord this simple question: How do I go forward from here?

_____

_____

_____

_____

_____

IN THE WORLD

I do not pray that You should take them out of the world,
but that You should keep them from the evil one.[1]
—JOHN 17:15

THE VERY CORE of Christ's prayer to the Father in John 17 was intercession. He wasn't focused on Himself and what He was about to face. Jesus prayed for the disciples. It is stunning and sobering that so shortly before Jesus was betrayed and brutalized, He was concerned for His disciples. We will never see a more perfect example of someone who emptied Himself and was concerned about the needs of others. Jesus had done all He physically could to equip and prepare the disciples before His crucifixion. So what did He do? He prayed.

IN, BUT NOT OF

Jesus prayed to the Father that the disciples would not be taken out of the world, but rather that they would be in the world and kept from the evil one who rules it. One of the greatest paradoxes of the Christian life is fully exposed in John 17:15: Christians are to be *in* the world, but not *of* the world. We are to live, work, and interact with others. We are to raise children, respect authorities, and be involved in our educational systems, business enterprises, and public affairs. At a distance it might appear we are just like nonbelievers in the world, but up close, when our values are challenged and our character is tested, people must see that our standards for living and our citizenship are not of this realm (Phil. 3:20). The industrious

Christian businessman who has proved to be a faithful steward of God's property recognizes that everything he possesses is a sacred stewardship from God. The Christian who governs in a position of secular authority understands that God has placed him there, not his own ingenuity or personal charisma.

Because we have been brought into the kingdom of heaven at salvation (Eph. 2:19–22; Col. 1:13), the principles by which we live now stand in stark contrast to everything in the world. But Jesus's prayer was we would be kept from the evil one while in the world. No matter how different we are as Christians, our charge will be to infiltrate the world's culture by being light and salt. However different the body of Christ is from other groups in the world, the church will never be sequestered physically or practically from the world. It will be intertwined in the very fabric of society. Jesus leaves us the perfect, practical example of how all of this is to be accomplished—He prays to the Father. It is in prayer that we will always discover God's answer to this crucial question: What does it mean to be *in*, but not *of*, the world?

There is no escaping the call of Christ on our lives to be in the world. We are brought into the kingdom of God to bring His kingdom to this earth. "The kingdom of God does not come with observation. Nor will they say, 'Here it is!' or 'There it is!' For remember, the kingdom of God is within you" (Luke 17:20–21). The kingdom of God is not some mystical place in the heavenly realm that is only enjoyed when our lives come to an end. We are God's agents of redemption in the lives of men, right now. Jesus came to set the captives free (Luke 4:18), and when He ascended to heaven, He gave that calling to His disciples. We now have this calling, and by the power of the Holy Spirit we will carry on His work (John 14:12).

KEPT FROM THE EVIL ONE

Jesus prays to the Father that He would "keep" us from the evil one. He makes this request because the world is the territory of the enemy. The world is where Satan has his influence and power (John 12:31; 14:30; 2 Cor. 4:4). Anyone who follows Christ in this world better be prepared for war (2 Tim. 3:12). The Bible means exactly what it says: "We know that we are of God, and that the whole world lies in the power of the evil one" (1 John 5:19, NASB).

But Jesus knows that the Father can save us from the evil one. Jesus, the man, spent hours and days in the Father's presence, praying, listening, and understanding the Father's character. He and the Father were one in the Holy Spirit. Jesus was confidently assured that He could pray to the Father and the Father would keep these disciples, and us, from any temptation the evil one puts in the path. The Word promises, "No temptation has taken you except what is common to man. God is faithful, and He will not permit you to be tempted above what you can endure, but will with the temptation also make a way to escape, that you may be able to bear it" (1 Cor. 10:13).

The enemy is cunning and full of schemes. He works in the shadows, in degrees of separation, in partial truths, and in compromises. What does it mean practically to be kept from the enemy's territory, the world? That little word *keep* elicits disagreement, division, and even anger among Christians. What are we to be kept from in the world? What is permissible or not permissible? Can we live lavish lifestyles while others hunger? Is it OK to have a retirement and savings account? Is it possible to live with one foot in each kingdom? There are so many questions and possible misunderstandings. But what about this one: Can we love the things in the world?

Love Is the Answer to All Questions

Let's be honest with ourselves—there are some very enticing items in the world. The pleasures of the world are luscious, delightful, beautiful, desirable, and even fun. The world is pervasive in its enticements, and it surrounds us every day with a barrage of temptations. Christ prayed we would be kept from the corruption and temptations of the world, that we wouldn't love the world. Love is the answer to all the questions we could ever raise about how we can be *in*, but not *of*, the world.

We are to love the Lord our God with all our hearts, and our neighbors as ourselves (Mark 12:29–31). We are to love others, even our enemies (Luke 6:35). But God's Word is very clear— we are not to love the things that are in the world. "Do not love the world or the things in the world. If anyone loves the world, the love of the Father is not in him. For all that is in the world—the lust of the flesh, the lust of the eyes, and the pride of life—is not of the Father, but is of the world" (1 John 2:15–16).

Does that mean you can't love going to the movies? What about your love for your favorite football team? The simple answer and the truth are lost in the soft Christianity of our day and the lukewarm church: we cannot love the world. This doesn't mean we can't possess nice things, enjoy going to a respectable movie, or live in a more-than-modest home. But when we start living our lives in pursuit of the same things that unbelievers run after, we are in very dangerous waters. So much boils down to that little word *love*.

A Special Word About Work

A proper understanding of the Christian's attitude regarding work is vitally important if we are going to live *in* the world without being *of* the world. Practically all of us are going to work most of our adult lives. How do we plunge into work, spending the bulk of our week at work, and not be consumed and burdened by the world? How do we go to work every day and not become like the world?

God has called us to "pray without ceasing" (1 Thess. 5:17). This includes every moment we are at work. For the Christian who is being sanctified by the Word of God, every task can become a prayer. "And whatever you do in word or deed, do all in the name of the Lord Jesus, giving thanks to God the Father through Him" (Col. 3:17). It makes no difference if our work is mundane or magnificent; we can do it for the Lord (Col. 3:23). And we can be salt and light in the world without being *of* the world.

WHEN YOU PRAY

The principles of the kingdom stand in stark contrast to the world.

Where are you most tempted to love the things of the world?

In quiet reflection ask the Lord to reveal the areas in which your heart is drawn to the world. Give Him plenty of wait time to speak to you.

_____

_____

_____

_____

_____

NOT OF THE WORLD

Sanctify them by Your truth. Your word is truth.
—JOHN 17:17

IN THE PRESENCE of the disciples Jesus prayed to the Father His most earnest desires for them. They are words that carry such dramatic spiritual truths for us. Jesus prayed that the disciples would be one with Him and the Father, and with one another; that they would not be taken from the world but saved from it; and that they would be sanctified.

Following Jesus is about making choices. We have to choose to come into the kingdom of heaven. There is a forsaking of the past and the world that only we can do as we make that purposeful decision to follow Christ. We have complete free will in this. We have to choose to accept the free gift that Christ offers us in salvation (Rom. 4:15–16). But when it comes to sanctification, there is no free gift. Christ does not freely give us character or sanctification. The choice to be consecrated for service to the Lord and to walk a holy life rests on our shoulders. However, though the choice is ours, we don't have the power to overcome the world, the flesh, and the devil. We are powerless in and of ourselves. The power to follow Christ in sanctification comes from the Holy Spirit.

DEATH AND SANCTIFICATION

Let's start with what sanctification is not. Sanctification is not a retooling of the old man. God's not interested in saving our natural lives. The great work that Jesus does in us at salvation is to give us a new heart, one that is soft and tender to the Lord and able to receive the promptings of the Holy Spirit. "No, a true Jew is one whose heart is right with God. And true circumcision is not merely obeying the letter of the law; rather, it is a change of heart produced by the Spirit. And a person with a changed heart seeks praise from God, not from people" (Rom. 2:29, NLT). God said, "I will give you a new heart, and a new spirit I will put within you. And I will take away the stony heart out of your flesh, and I will give you a heart of flesh" (Ezek. 36:26). What we do with this new heart is our choice to make.

If we make the purposeful choice to follow the Lord in sanctification, we draw a line in the sand with the enemy and the battle begins. You see, the enemy isn't disturbed about the nominal Christian who seldom prays and doesn't mature into a disciple. This person is no threat to the world Satan rules. But the disciple who prays and decides to pursue the fullness of the Lord found in sanctification poses a great threat to all the enemy stands for.

I think we take this whole issue of sanctification way too flippantly. Sanctification can be a violent process. The enemy doesn't like it, and our flesh rails against it. There is nothing pretty about dying to yourself. Through sanctification the Spirit of God is putting His finger on every aspect of our lives that is not in concert with His purposes. Sanctification is taking everything that captures our attention on this earth and putting it through a filter that allows only those things that interest God to pass through.

Life and Sanctification

Sanctification is finding the oneness with Christ that He prayed for in John 17. All that represents my natural life— my degrees, job title, experience, status, and so on—must diminish through sanctification. What increases instead is everything that interests God. There is a mystifying transaction that takes place in sanctification. The Spirit of God reduces me to who I am and nothing else—no false identities, no masks, no achievements, no anything. I then step into the understanding that Jesus is my sanctification. "But because of Him you are in Christ Jesus, whom God made unto us wisdom, righteousness, sanctification, and redemption" (1 Cor. 1:30). I don't have to try to mimic Jesus; rather, the character of Christ's life is displayed through me.

Sanctified Through the Truth

God has given us everything we need to live a sanctified life (2 Pet. 1:3). We have a personal guide to show us the way— God's Word, the truth. In the Word I am taught how to come to know God. In the Word I am taught how to pray. The Holy Spirit will even teach me how to receive the Word of God into my life.

Prayer needs fuel to ignite it. God's Word is that fuel. In the parable of the soils the seed in the good soil were those who heard the Word with an honest and good heart (Luke 8:15). The truth of God placed in our hearts will reap a reward of righteousness: "Commit your way to the LORD; trust also in Him, and He will bring it to pass. He will bring forth your righteousness as the light, and your judgment as the noonday" (Ps. 37:5–6). He is the One who brings forth our righteousness. Hear this now: Sanctification isn't our responsibility. It is God's. Our role is simply to dedicate ourselves to God and keep a good heart (Prov. 4:23).

The good news is that we can come to the Lord in prayer and the Holy Spirit will provide in-the-moment counseling. He will let us know what really demands our love. The Word of God points us in the right direction: sanctification—becoming more like God and less like the world. As this happens in our lives, we find the understanding to live in the world without being *of* the world. We are living in the kingdom of God.

PRAYING THE SCRIPTURES

Every one of us needs to learn how to pray Scripture. It is a vital part of where we find direction, our personal sanctification, and how we engage in spiritual warfare. Jesus rebuffed temptation with Scripture (Matt. 4:4). God is committed to the promises He gives us in the Word (2 Chron. 6:14–15). We build our faith by praying the Word (Rom. 10:17). In praying the Scriptures, the first thing we are seeking is God's presence and fellowship. We are giving God time to reveal Himself to us. Praying the Scriptures is simply reading a passage and asking God in prayer what He wants to speak to us.

The Word of God and prayer are eternally linked. The Word not only teaches me who I am in Christ but also reveals all the magnificent acts God will do for me. Through praying with the Word of God, I am able to understand who I can be in Christ.

When You Pray

God's will is that I be sanctified.

Identify a few areas of life where you have yet to encounter freedom.

Find a few scriptures that relate to those areas, and pray them today and in the weeks to come. It is always God's will for you to be free.

_____

_____

_____

_____

_____

_____

_____

_____

_____

_____

_____

_____

_____

_____

WATCH AND PRAY

Then Jesus came with them to a place called Gethsemane and said to the disciples, "Sit here while I go and pray close by." . . . Then He came to the disciples and found them sleeping, and said to Peter, "So, could you not keep watch with Me one hour? Watch and pray that you enter not into temptation. The spirit indeed is willing, but the flesh is weak."[1]
—MATTHEW 26:36, 40–41

H OW MUCH TIME in prayer is sufficient? Fifteen minutes? Thirty minutes? An hour?

I made a decision to dedicate time to the Lord in prayer and the Word. However, my schedule was overfull, and there seemed to be no free time. I was a father with five children. As a high school principal I was at the school by 6:45 a.m. every weekday and had activities often three nights weekly. I had a second job from 3:45 a.m. to 5:00 a.m. seven days a week so my wife could stay at home to homeschool our children. Then there were the responsibilities at my church as an elder. I told the Lord there was simply no time to pray in the middle of all this busyness. What could be done? As clearly as if He had written it on the wall, His answer came: "You have time to pray."

I cried out to the Lord for strength and decided to set aside 5:15 a.m. to 6:15 a.m. (one little hour) every day to pray and study. Honestly it was a painful discipline at first. However, in a short number of months it became a great joy and blessing to my life. I started listening in quiet for the Lord to speak through His Word. I prayed for others and meditated on Scripture. What started out as a burden turned into the most glorious time of spiritual growth in my life. Because I was so busy and had so much to accomplish, I could not afford to miss my morning time in Christ's presence. And what happened was as unexplainable as it was mystical. Morning after morning it was as if the clock moved at a snail's pace. Time seemed to stand still. So much of the Word and prayer were deposited in my life during those early morning hours.

ONE HOUR

Jesus was distressed and troubled, and He needed the disciples to watch with Him in prayer. He had modeled prayer, and now it was time for them to support Him in prayer.

What happened next is one of those encounters in the Scriptures when we see our Lord's humanity so clearly it can't be denied. At one point He is the humble Son of Man who has sat peacefully with His disciples at a last meal. He did this knowing He was going to be betrayed and knowing the great grief and distress that would befall Him in the garden. Then in the garden Christ was suffering in His soul, the sorest of all sufferings. He had to wrestle with the emotions of being betrayed; He had to contemplate the ensuing crucifixion and the ultimate struggle in His will, knowing that the decision was His alone. Jesus would choose to be made a curse for us. He would taste death by crucifixion and its great bitterness. He experienced the natural fear of pain, suffering, and death. Christ the man pleaded with His Father—if it is possible, remove this suffering.

With all this in mind, surely the disciples could pray for one hour. I mean, it was just one hour. It is easy to jump to the conclusion that the disciples were just physically weak or spiritually out of step with the Lord. One hour does not seem like an unrealistic request. However, they were just men—men who were experiencing great emotional unrest and a harrowing schedule with little rest.

Still, can you hear the Lord's stinging rebuke in just these few words: "Could you not keep watch with Me one hour?" (Matt. 26:40)? He finds them sleeping three different times when they should have been praying. The hour is coming that Jesus is being betrayed, and they are sleeping.

Jesus then speaks words that describe so many of us in prayer: "The spirit indeed is willing, but the flesh is weak" (v. 41). Our intentions are good. We know it is a great idea to pray. We know we can discover the answers to our problems in prayer. If we can just pray consistently, it will all turn around. All of these statements could be true. However, what we commonly experience in prayer is that our words seem to run out quickly because we do not know the discipline of prayer. We are praying in the flesh.

THE WIND OF THE HOLY SPIRIT

When we pray in the flesh, we are like couch potatoes trying to run a marathon—we are winded and simply do not have what it takes to finish. When we pray, we must pray in the Spirit. It is the Spirit who provides the strength and the energy to pray. The Spirit, *pneuma* in the Greek, is more properly termed "breath" or "wind."[2] When the Holy Spirit filled the disciples on the Day of Pentecost, "a sound like a mighty rushing wind came from heaven, and it filled the whole house where they were sitting" (Acts 2:2).

Just like the couch potato trying to run, our flesh has no

strength and no breath, but the powerful wind of the Holy Spirit fills us and gives us the strength and breath we need to pray. It is the encouragement that Paul gives in Ephesians 6:18: "Pray in the Spirit always with all kinds of prayer and supplication. To that end be alert with all perseverance and supplication for all the saints." By praying in the Spirit, we can finish the marathon of life without running out of breath. We can persevere. We can develop the discipline of prayer. We can "run with endurance the race that is set before us" (Heb. 12:1).

When You Pray

Even though your flesh is weak, the Holy Spirit will strengthen and energize you in prayer.

How much time do you spend in prayer daily? What about weekly?

What needs to be removed from your life in order to make more room for the Holy Spirit?

Pray and ask the Lord to fill you with the wind of the Holy Spirit so you can run your race with endurance.

PERSEVERING PRAYER

*Then Jesus came with them to a place called Gethsemane and said
to the disciples, "Sit here while I go and pray close by." . . . He said to
them, "My soul is very sorrowful, even to death. Wait here, and keep
watch with Me." . . . He prayed, "O My Father, if it is possible, let
this cup pass from Me. Nevertheless, not as I will, but as You will."
Then He came to the disciples and found them sleeping, and
said to Peter, "So, could you not keep watch with Me one
hour? Watch and pray that you enter not into temptation. The spirit indeed is willing, but the flesh is weak."
He went away a second time and prayed, "O My Father, if this cup
cannot pass away from Me unless I drink it, Your will be done."
Again, He came and found them sleeping, for their eyes
were heavy. So leaving them again, He went away and
prayed the third time, saying the same words.[1]
—MATTHEW 26:36, 38–44*

*An angel from heaven appeared to Him, strengthening Him. And
being in anguish, He prayed more earnestly. And His sweat
became like great drops of blood falling down to the ground.
—LUKE 22:43–44*

ONE OF THE lessons about prayer our Lord repeatedly
taught is we must persevere. This may be the greatest
stumbling block to the prayer life of most Christians.
Answers to prayers don't come as quickly as we anticipate.
Let's be completely honest with ourselves here—patience
is not exactly something we practice a great deal in our

nanosecond-response-time culture. In my counseling with young people, I tell them lust isn't necessarily about sex. My definition of *lust* is "I want it, and I want it now!" If there is a sure prescription for failure in prayer, it is the attitude of "I want my answer, and I want it now." Our love of ease, impatience, and spiritual laziness don't contribute to persevering prayer.

PERSEVERANCE

Jesus declared very pointedly in the parable of the persistent widow and the judge that men should pray and not give up (Luke 18:1–8). What exactly is the perseverance that the widow displayed in this parable? I believe it includes intensity, courage, and patience that refuses to let up and quit pressing. This widow had a persistence about her that refused to take no for an answer.

But why doesn't God just go ahead and answer our prayers? That's a great question. God has an end game with us—an eternal, essential purpose. That purpose is oneness with Him and being conformed into His image. Above all things, including answering our prayers, He wants to draw us deeply into Him. Persisting in unanswered prayer is the training ground for increased faith. It's the place where God extends grace to us, and it is the perfect soil for character building. Unanswered prayer leaves us vulnerable before the Lord, the ideal place for surrender.

We all face discouragement with unanswered prayers. We must recognize when discouragement sets in, for it can lead to withdrawal—from praying, from concern for a particular prayer need, and potentially from fellowship with the Lord and others. We must consider that there is a reason for the delay of an answer to prayer or for the answer not being what we wanted it to be. And God knows exactly what it is. In the face of unanswered prayer we should always ask if we are praying according to the Word and God's will.

Our Helper

Our Lord was in great agony in the garden, but He persevered. Our Lord's suffering revealed His perfect oneness with the Father and the Holy Spirit. Only Luke records this scene, but it is critical that we understand the lesson here as Jesus agonized. "An angel from heaven appeared to Him, strengthening Him" (Luke 22:43). God never intended that we live the Christian life in our own strength or pray according to just our own will. The Holy Spirit and angelic hosts are ever present to support and encourage us. They helped Jesus as He prayed in the garden, and they will help us. As we abide in Christ, we learn to daily experience the right portion of Spirit-filled prayer and the Word to live the Spirit-filled life.

For us to experience persevering prayer, we must be filled with the Spirit—and it's not just a one-time filling, but an everyday filling. Paul exhorted us to "keep on being filled with the Spirit" (Eph. 5:18, ISV). The life of continual communion we desire will be unattainable unless we give ourselves to the indwelling of the Spirit, holding nothing back.

How does this happen? It is a waste of time to pray for the fullness of the Spirit and the power to persevere in prayer if you are not willing to have all facets of your life measured against the Word of God. If you haven't done this, then your prayers are futile. Christ is our example. He held nothing back, hid nothing, and had no backup plan, no exit strategy. Following Jesus daily demands nothing less from us. It calls for our passions, likes, dislikes, obsessions, addictions, biases, and all that encompasses our soul to be submitted to Him. Meeting the requirements of being disciples takes a powerful act of God in us through the Holy Spirit.

There are two truths to learn and practice about the Holy Spirit and prayer:

1. At the start of the day we must ask the Father for the Spirit.
2. We must then ask the Spirit to teach us and help us in our prayers, the reading of the Word, and our daily living.

It is through the Holy Spirit that we are able to have perseverance in prayer. It is through Him that we can live in prayer even while we work or go about our day. We can pray always. "Rejoice always. Pray without ceasing. In everything give thanks, for this is the will of God in Christ Jesus concerning you" (1 Thess. 5:16–18). Our launchpad for persevering is Spirit-led prayer. Be encouraged to "build yourselves up in your most holy faith. Pray in the Holy Spirit" (Jude 20).

WHEN YOU PRAY

You must learn to pray in the Holy Spirit and to pray with perseverance.

Practice this manner of prayer over the next few days in your prayer times: Remind yourself with scriptures that the Lord hears and answers your prayers (John 14:13–14; 15:7, 16; 16:23–26), and invite the Holy Spirit to be with you as you wait in silence. Then pray as the Spirit leads you.

As you do this for a few days, record what the Lord is teaching you through the Holy Spirit about praying in the Spirit.

_____

_____

_____

_____

_____

_____

_____

_____

_____

_____

_____

_____

_____

_____

_____

_____

_____

FORGIVING EVEN THE UNFORGIVABLE

Jesus said, "Father, forgive them, for they know not what they do." And they divided His clothes by casting lots.[1]
—LUKE 23:34

T HERE ARE ONLY a small number of spiritual truths you have to apply to your life to follow Christ in the fullness of the Spirit. Forgiveness is the linchpin of those truths. Salvation and our maturity into full-grown sons and daughters are predicated on forgiveness. At the end of Christ's earthly life He left a demonstration of forgiveness that authenticated for eternity the importance He placed on forgiving. One of the last phrases He spoke was, "Father, forgive them, for they know not what they do."

THE BONDAGE BREAKER

How many times must we forgive someone? Ten? Twenty? Seventy times seven? Jesus told the disciples, and in particular Peter, how important it is to break the bondage of unforgiveness with a brother, no matter how monumental the offense (Matt. 18:21–35). When Christ answered Peter's question about how many times he should forgive someone who sins against him, He gave an astounding, shocking answer: "up to seventy times seven" (v. 22). Now Jesus didn't mean to keep track of how many times someone sins against you so you could refuse to forgive the 491st sin. It is not about the numbers at all. His point is that we need to have a spirit of forgiveness. Jesus told a parable to illustrate His point.

> Therefore the kingdom of heaven is like a certain king who wanted to settle accounts with his servants. When he began to settle the accounts, one was brought to him who owed him ten thousand talents. But since he was not able to pay, his master ordered that he be sold with his wife, their children, and all that he had, and payment to be made.
>
> So the servant fell on his knees, pleading with him, saying, "Master, have patience with me, and I will pay you everything." Then the master of that servant was moved with compassion, released him, and forgave him the debt.
>
> But that same servant went out and found one of his fellow servants who owed him a hundred denarii. He laid hands on him and took him by the throat, saying, "Pay me what you owe."
>
> So his fellow servant fell down at his feet and entreated him, saying, "Have patience with me, and I will pay you everything."
>
> But he would not and went and threw him in prison until he should pay the debt. So when his fellow servants saw what took place, they were very sorry and went and told their master all that had taken place.
>
> Then his master, after he had summoned him, said to him, "O you wicked servant! I forgave you all that debt because you pleaded with me. Should you not also have had compassion on your fellow servant, even as I had pity on you?" His master was angry and delivered him to the jailers until he should pay all his debt.
>
> —MATTHEW 18:23–34

How serious is forgiveness? Jesus ends the parable by telling the disciples, "So also My heavenly Father will do to each of you, if from your heart you do not forgive your brother for his trespasses" (Matt. 18:35). Wow, that is serious!

If you don't give forgiveness, you don't receive forgiveness. Is it conceivable that our personal forgiveness of sins could be measured against our forgiveness of the offenses of others against us? If Jesus said it, He meant it. He said it emphatically in the Sermon on the Mount: "But if you do not forgive men for their sins, neither will your Father forgive your sins" (Matt. 6:15).

But there is more to it than that. Jesus's parable also illustrates that unforgiveness puts us in bondage. A heart full of unforgiveness and bitterness is a heart that is imprisoned. But it is "for freedom [that] Christ freed us. Stand fast therefore and do not be entangled again with the yoke of bondage" (Gal. 5:1). When we choose to forgive, we loose the chains of bondage that would keep us in prison to bitterness and resentment. Forgiveness is the bondage breaker.

MAKE FORGIVENESS A HABIT

One of my personal habits is to periodically ask the Lord if there is anyone I've offended. Is there anyone I need to forgive or seek forgiveness from? If so, it typically means going to the person and shouldering responsibility for my words or actions that may have precipitated an offense. During one of my recent early morning devotional times, I posed this question again to the Lord in prayer: Is there anyone I am separated from or I've offended? I did what any good educator does after he poses a question—I provided "wait time" to give the other person a chance to speak. I waited, and nothing came to my mind. A few days later I was reading a book, and the Lord got in the middle of it. I heard a name I hadn't thought of in years, Aunt Ruby. It was a God thought—one of those flickering electrical firings emitted from the Holy Spirit to a memory reservoir, unlocking it and bringing a thought back to your mind.

Several years ago my family had a bitter split when my grandparents passed away. There were accusations, hurtful words, and offenses enough to go around. Uncle Buddy and Aunt Ruby were two of my favorite relatives. I spent days with them growing up as a little boy. My uncle was one of my champions, a decorated war veteran with medals to prove it, a true hero. That nasty incident around the inheritances of my grandparents pitted "their" side of the family against "our" side. When I heard Aunt Ruby's name in my mind, I hearkened to the prayer time a few days before. I knew I had a phone call to make. It took me a day or two to muster the humility and write out my planned appeal for forgiveness. I had it all scripted so well. When I got Ruby on the phone, I froze and could only blurt out, "Please forgive me for not making this phone call years ago." Ruby immediately responded without missing a beat, "I am so glad you called." Her response disarmed the situation completely, and I proceeded to ask her forgiveness for my insensitivity and contribution to our family's division. We had a precious time of restoration.

Are there people for whom there is no hope of forgiveness? On the cross the first words that Christ spoke were a prayer, asking the Father to forgive His bitter enemies. None of us has ever suffered the kind of vile treatment that Christ received, yet He prayed for those who mistreated Him the most. The Romans demonstrated unparalleled cruelty, but Christ's prayer showed that there was hope even for the Romans. Dear friend, if you think there is no hope for someone for whom you have been interceding, take heart. "The Lord is not slow concerning His promise, as some count slowness. But He is patient with us, because He does not want any to perish, but all to come to repentance" (2 Pet. 3:9).

Have you ever had a true enemy, someone it seems has made it his mission to destroy your life? Have you been profoundly and deeply hurt by someone who is supposed to love you? Have you been victimized? How could you forgive such a person? How does our Lord tell us to deal with such a person? Jesus said, "Love your enemies, bless those who curse you, do good to those who hate you, and pray for those who spitefully use you and persecute you" (Matt. 5:44). How outrageous! Who could imagine such a thing? Yet it is the very example He left us on the cross. Forgiveness is making the choice to release yourself from bondage, leaving the one who sinned against you in the hands of the Father. So shake off the dust of the past and the sins that were committed against you, arise as a child of God, and loose yourself from the bonds of unforgiveness (Isa. 52:2). Choose to walk in the freedom to which you have been called (Gal. 5:13), for "where the Spirit of the Lord is, there is freedom" (2 Cor. 3:17, NIV).

PREPARATION FOR PRAYER

There is a preparation for prayer that is essential. That preparation hinges on forgiveness. It is the prayer of the righteous person that is effective with God. The prayer of an unrighteous man may be effective with man. Eloquent words with emotional appeals may move men, but it is the fervent prayer of a righteous man that moves God. The Bible states clearly, "Confess your faults to one another and pray for one another, that you may be healed. The effective, fervent prayer of a righteous man accomplishes much" (James 5:16).

Where does this righteousness come from? A person cannot

make himself or herself holy. When we trust in Christ, we have the power of the Holy Spirit to enable us to live more righteous lives. We have the power to overcome sin. This transformation is not something we do—it is completely a work of God. Our part is to repent of our sins and confess Jesus as Savior.

This great forgiveness and the power of the Holy Spirit empower us to follow Christ as disciples. Christ gave great promises to those who keep His commandments: "If you love Me, keep My commandments. I will pray the Father, and He will give you another Counselor, that He may be with you forever" (John 14:15–16) and "If you remain in Me, and My words remain in you, you will ask whatever you desire, and it shall be done for you" (John 15:7). It is in this state that we find ourselves clothed with the garments of salvation and wrapped in the robes of righteousness. We become men and women who can move heaven and earth through prayer to bless others.

WHEN YOU PRAY

Seek forgiveness quickly, and give forgiveness liberally.

In your quiet time today ask Jesus if there is anyone toward whom you are harboring unforgiveness.

If the Holy Spirit brings a name to your mind, share this with someone close to you, and ask him or her to pray for you. Ask the Holy Spirit to help you forgive and to set you free from the bonds of unforgiveness.

_____

_____

_____

DAY 37

FORSAKEN BUT PRAYING

And at the ninth hour Jesus cried out with a loud voice,
saying, "Eloi, Eloi, lama sabachthani?" which means, "My
God, My God, why have You forsaken Me?" [1]
—MARK 15:34

My GOD, My God, why have you forsaken me?" Have you ever felt forsaken by the Lord? Abandoned? It is a lonely feeling to find yourself in the middle of a crisis or situation you can't explain or do anything about. Can you trust Him with all the challenging events of life and live in faith? Even in the midst of suffering and pain? We must come to the conclusion and understanding that the Lord uses all things to accomplish His purposes in our lives. Prayer must be real with no pretense. We need to be reminded that the purpose of prayer is to develop a relationship of intimacy with our Lord. Intimacy demands honesty, which in these kinds of circumstances means crying out to the Lord just as Jesus did with His Father.

WHEN YOU FEEL ABANDONED

Jesus claimed God as His Father, yet He lamented that the Father was withdrawing His love and care for Him. The Father abandoned Christ while Christ bore our sins on the cross. It was the greatest price that could be paid for our sin, Christ's suffering. Though forsaken, Christ remained faithful to His mission—redemption for those who would choose salvation through Him.

John the Baptist was in prison, not knowing that he would be beheaded. He sent his disciples to Jesus to ask if He was the Messiah, or if they should look for another. Jesus responded, "Go and tell John what you have seen and heard: that the blind see, the lame walk, the lepers are cleansed, the deaf hear, the dead are raised, and the gospel is preached to the poor. Blessed is he who does not fall away on account of Me" (Luke 7:22–23). If there was ever a man who should receive the Lord's full blessing, it was John. From an early age John took the vow of a Nazarite and dedicated his life to God. He denied his flesh as much as any man who lived. Yet John's life ended with doubt about Christ's identity; he perhaps wondered if he had given his life in vain as he sat in prison. The man had questions yet was told, "Blessed is he who does not fall away on account of Me." I have no doubt that John, upon hearing the wondrous things his disciples had heard and seen, knew the answer to his question. Yes, Jesus was the coming One; they should look for no other. John remained true, trusting Jesus with his life until the end.

I know a couple who are the epitome of godly people—they mentor and pour their lives into others like few Christians I have ever known. Their youngest daughter was the worship leader at the Christian school where I was headmaster. She was a beautiful, talented, zealous, anointed Christian girl. The first time I saw her was in a church service when she was twelve years old. She was prophesying. After she graduated from our school, she attended a Christian college to study nursing. Shortly after her first semester of college, she was tragically killed in a car accident. Many years before, the same family had lost its only son in a tragic accident and later had a stillborn child. If ever people had cause to become disillusioned and lose their faith, this couple did. Yet they are full of the Spirit of our Lord, humble, peaceable, and joyous.

There will be times in life when you feel abandoned. The burden may seem more than is humanly possible to bear. We want to ask why these events happen, but *why?* isn't the right question. The right question is, will you worship and follow God even if He does not meet your expectations? Will you follow Him even when you feel forsaken?

Christ is our model. No one paid a greater price. He cast off His divinity to become a man and die for the sin of the world. Even when Jesus felt forsaken, He obeyed His heavenly Father with boundless joy and inordinate suffering. "But God demonstrates His own love toward us, in that while we were yet sinners, Christ died for us" (Rom. 5:8).

THE DANGER OF DISAPPOINTMENT

We know that disappointment can be a serious problem. Through hardships, personal failures, accidents, betrayal, afflictions, unmet expectations, and many other apparently negative experiences, we can lose sight of God's purposes and plan. When we don't see how the Lord weaves all our experiences into His purpose in our lives, we often respond in disappointment. Disappointment leads to self-pity, disillusionment, depression, and even withdrawal from fellowship.

We need to remember that His purpose for disappointment is to reproduce His character in us, for us to empty ourselves of our spirit and fully take in His Spirit. Affliction hems us in. We become so confined that we have no other option but Jesus. "Our light affliction, which lasts but for a moment, works for us a far more exceeding and eternal weight of glory, while we do not look at the things which are seen, but at the things which are not seen. For the things which are seen are temporal, but the things which are not seen are eternal" (2 Cor. 4:17–18). Through it all we can choose Jesus or respond with disappointment. The psalmist said, "Before I was afflicted I wandered, but now I keep Your word" (Psalm 119:67).

Jesus was our example, and He gave thanks in all things. He trusted the character of God, knowing that His Father was always at work. In the face of disappointment we need to find the place where we can give thanks because we trust God. We can be confident that the Lord will achieve His purposes for our lives and that all things will be woven into His master plan. "For from Him and through Him and to Him are all things. To Him be glory forever! Amen" (Rom. 11:36).

So will you continue to praise and serve Him when He does not meet your expectations? Even when you feel forsaken, will you choose to trust that God is working everything for your good? Will you continue in prayer?

WHEN YOU PRAY

Continue in prayer no matter the circumstance, even and especially when you feel forsaken.

What situation are you facing that is challenging you to the core of your soul to continue in prayer?

Consider sharing this with someone, and ask him or her to stand in prayer with you for answered prayer.

_____

_____

_____

DAY 38

DESTINATION

And Jesus cried out with a loud voice, "Father, into Your hands I commit My spirit." Having said this, He gave up the spirit.[1]
—LUKE 23:46

JESUS WAS ON a mission. Before the foundation of the world plans were laid out for the redemption of mankind. Jesus was to be the Way of that redemption. He came forth from the Godhead to earth, lived and died as a man, and in the process brought salvation to fallen man. He returned to heaven to be seated at the right hand of God and ever intercedes for us. Jesus knew exactly where He had come from, what He had to do, and where He was going.

Jesus never experienced identity crises. He didn't wonder if His life would have significance or make a difference. He didn't look to others for His sense of self-worth. He wasn't trying to please the multitudes. He didn't relish His influence with the crowds or their acclaim. Jesus wasn't influenced by what religious leaders thought of Him. He knew exactly what He was doing and where He was going. His life was lived for the approval of the only One who mattered, the Father.

CHARTING YOUR DESTINATION

If you have been with a man in a car, then you have ended up lost at some point. I have had more than my fair share of these embarrassing sidetracks. Men have this "special" thing going in their lives—it's called *pride*. It keeps us from listening to someone who knows where the destination is—in particular if that someone is a woman. It keeps us from stopping and looking at directions on the smartphone. So how do you get to the destination when you don't know the way?

Early in my career I managed admissions and financial aid at a Christian university, so I was around many college students. It seemed that numerous students had no earthly idea of their course of study or what they were going to do with their lives after college. One of the constant complaints I heard from students was about choosing a major. In many cases the choice was haphazard, influenced by others, selected because of ease, or even chosen because a particular major had the greatest lifetime earning potential. Really? When asked about their major, students who hadn't chosen one would say anything except that pitiful, degrading, disillusioning word *undecided*—clearly that's how they viewed being undecided. And when they did decide on a major, it was as if one of the great cathartic moments of their lives had just happened. All of life's challenges melted into insignificance in one swooping decision—by choosing a college major, purpose in life was discovered. Of course, forget that about 80 percent of students end up changing their major at least once.[2] How do Christian young people find their way?

If you read business journals or money magazines, you will see article after article about the monetary crises faced today upon retirement. It is called the greatest financial retirement crisis in the history of our nation. However, the financial crisis is nothing compared with the identity crises so many encounter. Many retirees face this stark question every morning: "Who am I now?" How do they find their way?

Rerouting to the Destination

We don't have to go the wrong way down a one-way street, turn repeatedly into a cul-de-sac, get off at the wrong exit, head in the wrong direction, or go around the mountain repeatedly for forty years. We don't have to wander around lost, with no sense of direction.

Jesus chose His destination—the cross. Many people think about Jesus's death on the cross and His resurrection; however, they don't conceptualize that Jesus is a living person in heaven. Jesus thinks about each one of us every day. He can handle that. He is part of the Godhead. He wants to be in relationship with us. He wants to guide us every day. To this end He has given us His Word and prayer. They are inseparable.

So how do we find our destination? The Holy Spirit shows us the way through the Word and prayer. As we submit our lives and futures to Christ, the Holy Spirit goes to work. He gives us clarity in our souls to have fellowship with God. The Holy Spirit reveals the pathway to have fellowship with Christ, keep His commandments, and abide in His love. The result? Our eyes are opened to the destination. The Lord says, "I will instruct you and teach you in the way you should go; I will counsel you with my eye on you" (Ps. 32:8). This verse means that the Lord will guide us, point us in the right direction, and then watch over us to keep us on course. Wow!

You Have Arrived at the Destination

Kelly wandered around lost as a kid in college—undecided. Wouldn't you know it, she dropped out of school. Then she bounced from job to job. She wanted to be successful but just couldn't find the right path. The truth is that in her failures she was being guided by the Lord—she would say she was being set up. She was on her way to His destination.

With no other place to turn, she felt led of the Lord to go to a particular city in Mexico by herself. Nuevo Laredo, Tamaulipas, Mexico, is a small border town with a "zone of tolerance"—a walled compound full of a range of brothels, bars, restaurants, and small stores where everything is legal, including drugs and prostitution. The compound's name is Boys Town.

For one and a half years Kelly prayer-walked the perimeter of Boys Town. That is all she knew to do. Just entering the threshold of the district was unsafe. Finally she said to the Lord, "I'll cross that threshold and go anyplace I am invited." Over the next months she befriended many prostitutes and store owners at their invitation.

One day in Boys Town a man she had never met came frantically running up to her. He said there was a girl who was sick and asking for her. Nervously she followed him as he went behind a bar, through an alley, and through a maze of balconies. In the back room of a dimly lit brothel, she found a very sick prostitute she had befriended. The girl pleaded for Kelly to pray for her. She prayed for the girl's healing. When Kelly opened her eyes, the girl's eyes were open, and she thanked Kelly for praying for her. But all Kelly could see was the face of Jesus in this woman. All she could feel was the love Christ must have for His lost daughter. Kelly was overwhelmed with emotion. She experienced His deep love for the unlovely. She encountered Jesus in a distressing disguise. She arrived at His destination for her. For the next several years she ministered to the unlovely, reaching those no one else could reach and serving the poor, diseased, and addicted.

"Father, into Your hands I commit My spirit." Jesus knew His destination. He finished the course. It is the very same for us. Whether it is in the day of trouble or at the end of our lives, as followers of Jesus we have the guarantee of the Father's watchfulness over us. We find safety in the Father's hands. Whether in Michigan or Mexico, He keeps watch over His own: "For in the time of trouble He will hide me in His pavilion; in the shelter of His tabernacle He will hide me; He will set me up on a rock" (Ps. 27:5).

Jesus's oneness with the Father was a great place of safety and security for Him. It gave Him the perfect humility and freedom to reach out and serve others: "Jesus, knowing that the Father had given all things into His hands and that He came from God and was going to God, rose from supper, laid aside His garments, and took a towel and wrapped Himself. After that, He poured water into a basin and began to wash the disciples' feet and to wipe them with the towel with which He was wrapped" (John 13:3–5).

All true service to God must come out of this kind of brokenness and humility. This humility is only found in the secret place in prayer as we come face-to-face with our God. We can have only one response to encountering our Lord in such intimacy—to be broken and humble. Here is where we too find the freedom to serve out of a pure heart, knowing that we are securely on the way to our divinely appointed destination.

In Christ's physical brokenness He found the freedom to even release control of His spirit. It was the ultimate act of trust. As we encounter the Lord in times of prayer, we too can come to know the Father in such a tender, trusting manner. We can give it all up, release control of our lives, and hold nothing back. He knows where we are, where we are going, and how we are going to get there.

WHEN YOU PRAY

There is peace in knowing where you're going.

Take a moment to write down a few of your goals in life, whether personal or spiritual.

Submit your goals to the Lord, and invite the Holy Spirit to speak to your heart and keep you on His course for your life.

_____

_____

_____

_____

_____

_____

_____

_____

_____

_____

AN INVITATION TO INTIMACY

As He sat at supper with them, He took the bread, blessed it and broke it, and gave it to them. Then their eyes were opened, and they recognized Him. And He vanished out of their sight.[1]
—LUKE 24:30–31

WHAT IS IT about sharing a meal? Jesus placed much value on it and conducted much of His ministry around it. Some of His meals were scandalous, such as the dinner with Levi and his questionable friends (Luke 5:27–32). Some meals must have been quite uncomfortable for the attendees, such as the supper at the house of a Pharisee (Luke 7:36–50). Most of His meals were intimate encounters, while others were momentous events during which He fed thousands.

Jesus made meals more than just about food; He made them divine encounters. So much of what He shared in these encounters seemed to come out serendipitously, but we know nothing happened by accident with Jesus. He was a man on a mission. He was always teaching. And of course He always began these times with others at the table with prayer. Everything in his life began with prayer.

THE TABLE

Prayer is the place where all facets of life come together for us as Christians. Everything fits. We encounter the Lord's presence, discern His direction for our lives, and call down God's blessing on others. Sharing a meal together is the most perfect of all places for us to encounter the fullness of the Lord with others in authentic fellowship. The demands of this experience touch the very depths of our lives in the most crucial areas.

Unity

We have learned that unity is not optional if we want to fully experience all God has for us in fellowship. There is a divine indifference we must have to our own agenda. When we come together to share a meal, we pray first and call on the Holy Spirit to empower us to lay down all our preconceptions, judgments, and persuasions. We bless the food and our fellowship. Fellowship, that spiritual, enigmatic, and fragile experience, awaits us if we can give ourselves to unity. Few things challenge us more to empty ourselves than the call to unity around the table.

Forgiveness

The communion table of our Lord begins with forgiveness. We are instructed to take a long look at the state of our hearts toward others before we partake of the Lord's Supper (1 Cor. 11:28). In the same way we will never encounter the richness of fellowship at the table of sustenance without an evaluation of our forgiveness quotient toward those present. As much as bread feeds our bodies, forgiveness feeds our souls. Keeping forgiveness in our prayers before meals is applying the salve of the Holy Spirit to our wounds. We become whole beings, able to communicate from a position of honesty and openness.

Gratitude

Every time we sit down for a meal, we should express gratefulness in prayer to the Lord. He is the giver of all good gifts. A simple meal is a daily reminder of the Lord's sacrifice for our salvation. At the table we are bound together with those who have also partaken of Jesus, the Bread of Life. While we may be consuming physical bread that is perishable, we are reminded of the imperishable Bread of Life and that we are recipients of this miraculous present. We are truly blessed: "Blessed is he who shall eat bread in the kingdom of God!" (Luke 14:15).

Humility

Sharing a meal together is a potent opportunity to exercise humility. True brotherly service occurs as we prefer others above ourselves. The acts of humility are small but a spiritual and physical reality around a meal. Allowing someone to eat first, taking the smaller portion of meat, or permitting someone to indulge in the only second helping all are concrete acts of being concerned for the needs of others.

Another very tangible way to practice humility around the table is to practice listening. The most palpable service we can offer a brother or sister at mealtime is to be quiet. Not allowing a brother or sister the opportunity to speak around the table is sending the clear message that "what I have to say is more important than what you have to say."

SHARING LIFE

Sharing meals together should be about sharing our lives. The table of our Lord was a place of intimacy and action for the early disciples. "And continuing daily with one mind in the temple, and breaking bread from house to house, they ate their food with gladness and simplicity of heart, praising God and having favor with all the people. And the Lord added to the church daily those who were being saved" (Acts 2:46–47).

Sharing the meal is an invitation to family. It is an invitation to be known and an invitation to be cared for. It is so much more than just a customary act. We share the day and what is happening in our lives. The experience of the early church should be the same experience we have today. There is so much that takes place around the table that can't happen in the formal church setting. As with many of the right things to do, we must fight for the time to sit down over a meal as families, as home fellowships, and as members of the body of Christ. Great encouragement awaits us as we eat a meal together. With glad and sincere hearts we encounter the Lord in a safe place.

One of the church movements today in the United States is constructed around creating small house churches. These house churches grow until they reach a point in numbers where they divide and continue to meet and reproduce. House churches are small groups of believers who meet weekly to pray and worship. These house churches have two major purposes: to produce disciples and to reach out to non-believers in the communities where they meet. Every time the house churches meet, they pray and worship. But there is a third element every time they meet—they share a meal together. Sharing a meal together is an invitation to intimacy.

JESUS SHOWS UP

Imagine the men traveling with this stranger. The three of them probably moved slower and slower as Jesus opened their understanding to the prophets foretelling of the Messiah. He even chided them for their foolishness of being slow of heart to believe all that the prophets said of the coming Savior.

Jesus would have gone further, but they begged Him to stay because it was nearly night. "Stay with us," they urged (Luke 24:29). They were in the place where their actions met God's promises. If we will seek Him, we will find Him. "You shall seek Me and find Me, when you shall search for Me with all your heart" (Jer. 29:13). He answers prayer when we persist. It really does all come down to this. Will we stand? Will we cry out? If we persist, if we continue in prayer, He will answer. If we can't be budged from the place of prayer, we will see great answers to prayer. Just as the men on the road to Emmaus, we can invite Jesus into the most common places of our lives, and He will show up. We bless a simple meal together, and He turns it into an opportunity to share our lives, with Him at the center.

When You Pray

Sharing a meal is always an invitation to pray and experience authentic fellowship with others.

Find a quiet place, turn off or get away from all technology, and wait quietly on the Lord in complete silence for ten to fifteen minutes. Ask the Holy Spirit to open your spiritual eyes about the times you share meals with those you love and other believers. Write down what the Lord shows you.

A FAMILIAR PLACE

Then He led them out as far as Bethany, and He
lifted up His hands and blessed them.[1]
—LUKE 24:50

JESUS LED THEM to Bethany. It was so familiar to Him. His time on earth would be finished where it all began. However, there is another very familiar action taking place: He started His ministry in prayer at the baptism and now will ascend to heaven while blessing His disciples in prayer. He began and ended His time on the earth in prayer.

FAMILIARITY WITH PRAYER

Prayer was as natural to Jesus as breathing. It is the pivotal lesson we must learn and the habit that should dominate our lives. Prayer is a natural part of the Christian life—we can live in a spirit of prayer in any circumstance.

If we were taught to pray as children, we would be so much more familiar and comfortable with prayer as adults. As headmaster of a Christian academy my encouragement to all teachers was to pray with students. In particular I wanted elementary teachers to pray in front of children and give them opportunities to pray. And while I worked with many outstanding Christian teachers throughout the years, one stands out when it comes to prayer: Jeanne. A few years ago she was diagnosed with stage IV lung cancer, even though she had never smoked. Jeanne said she lived in a Holy Spirit bubble as individuals from around the world interceded for her while she received medical treatment. Then a miracle occurred—within a year the invading cancer in several parts of her body was gone. However, fifteen months later a PET scan revealed the cancer was back. Initially her oncologist wasn't sure what the next step would be.

Jeanne is a woman of prayer. It permeates her life and thoughts. On numerous occasions she talked about the power of prayer with her ten- and eleven-year-old students. One day a boy raised his hand and asked if the class could pray for her. Jeanne said yes and asked one of the girls to do so. That is not what the class had in mind. Many of the students wanted the opportunity that only one was given. She fought weeping in their presence as they prayed for her one by one. It was incredibly special and humbling. Jeanne was confident that God listened not only to their words but also to their hearts. He answered their prayers. God touched her again. Today, after more than two years, she is vibrant, strong, and passionate about Jesus as she continues to manage only traces of cancer in her body. God divinely intervened in Jeanne's life, physically and spiritually, through the believing hearts of children who were accustomed to prayer. It was not unfamiliar territory for them. We must become like little children.

THE BLESSING

What was this blessing that Jesus gave to them? Whatever He said, it caused the disciples to stop and worship Him. Then they returned to Jerusalem with great joy—not just joy, but *great* joy! How could these disciples, who had been through so much with Him, leave that place full of joy, even after Jesus had vanished to heaven?

Jesus had authority, and now it was going to be bestowed on them. Jesus told them before they started out to Bethany that the Father was going to send what had been promised, the Holy Spirit, and they would be clothed with power from on high. All power belonged to Jesus, and He was bestowing it on them. In a short time they would engage the most powerful force in the universe, Spirit-empowered prayer. How could they not be filled with unspeakable joy?

The Beginning, Not the End

The blessing Jesus gave them was a blessing to begin the work to which He had called them. His ascension was their beginning. Today we must take Christ's ascension as the very foundation of His influence on the world. The disciples were soon to be filled with the Spirit and to be endued with power to go everywhere proclaiming the Word.

Jesus's final act of blessing His friends and disciples showed again His perfect oneness with the Father. Jesus was calling these disciples to their destiny—the Father's business of reconciling men to God. The power of the Holy Spirit in prayer was essential for their fulfillment of this quest.

One of the great lessons of Jesus's life is that He imparted a spirit of prayer to the disciples and all those who followed Him. His life communicated prayer. His life bestowed prayer on the disciples. Jesus made a life of prayer a priority in His limited time as a man. He imparted knowledge on prayer. In parables He taught us how to pray. He told us where to pray. He even taught what to pray.

Those of us in the teaching profession recognize that there are many ingredients that make an effective teacher. Nonetheless, no matter how many pedagogical theories or strategies emerge, the greatest and most effective method that teachers identify is example, example, and example. Jesus's life was the supreme example of prayer.

My wife's brother, Paul, lived to serve others, in particular at-risk boys. He spent a lifetime giving himself to Royal Rangers, the Assemblies of God youth program focused on introducing young boys to the outdoors and Christ. Through hundreds, if not thousands, of campouts, fishing trips, rock-climbing trips, nature hikes, campfires, and Bible studies, he touched the lives of thousands of young men deeply for Christ. His funeral was an amazing testimony to a life well lived. It has been said that only those things done for Christ will stand through time. Paul left many men standing for Jesus.

At Paul's funeral my wife told a story about Paul's grandson. During the last years of Paul's life he watched his little grandson a few days a week. One of Paul's habits was to bring a cool bottle of water out to the trash collectors when they came. A few days after Paul's untimely death his grandson was in his own home with his mom. The garbage truck could be heard coming down the street. Paul's grandson ran to his mom and insisted they get some bottles of water from the refrigerator to take out to the trash collectors. Oh, the power of example. A living example imparts its very life to others. "So having great love toward you, we were willing to impart to you not only the gospel of God but also our own lives, because you were dear to us" (1 Thess. 2:8). Jesus's life was a living example of prayer.

HIS LEGACY—OUR LEGACY

Because we have many different gifts and unique parts to play in Christ's church, we will leave a variety of legacies. However, there is clearly one great legacy open to all of us. I believe it is one to which we all should aspire. Let this be our prayer, Lord: "May the legacy of our lives be answered prayer, as was Yours."

He taught us when to pray, where to pray, how to pray, what to pray, the secret of prayer, the hindrances to prayer, how to use the Word in prayer, how to call down His blessing on others, how to be childlike in prayer, how to ask for the impossible, where to be trained for prayer, the key to opening the door to His greatest possibilities in prayer, how to intercede for others, how to experience the greatest power in prayer (unity), where to turn for help in prayer, how to live in a spirit of prayer, and how to experience the Holy Spirit in prayer. He holds nothing back from us.

There are so many things that vie for your time and put pressure on you: your job, family, bills, relationships, church commitments, and so many more. The message is simple yet profound and sure. You can build your entire life around prayer. Give yourself to it, and He will take care of the rest.

WHEN YOU PRAY

Jesus wants your legacy to be answered prayer.

Commit to writing down your "great requests" in prayer. Date them when you write them down, and record the date when they are answered. Begin today to chronicle your legacy of answered prayer.

_____

_____

_____

EPILOGUE

THE PRAYER LIFE of Christ is majestic and mysterious. Nothing reveals this more than the truth that there is no conclusion or ending to His prayers. There is no epilogue. Why? He always prays. It is His lasting ministry. There is no secret to what He is about right now in heaven. He lives to make intercession for us. He prays continually.

> But He, because He lives forever, has an everlasting priesthood. Therefore He is able to save to the uttermost those who come to God through Him, because He at all times lives to make intercession for them.
>
> —HEBREWS 7:24–25

> Who is he who condemns? It is Christ who died, yes, who is risen, who is also at the right hand of God, who also intercedes for us.
>
> —ROMANS 8:34

Jesus now sits in the position of authority, at the right hand of God. He spoke directly to the disciples that this would be His destination: "From now on the Son of Man will be seated at the right hand of the power of God" (Luke 22:69). He is interceding for us and doing what He modeled for us to do while He was on earth. Jesus has been praying continually.

His intercession gives us the great confidence to believe that there is no stronghold so impenetrable, no discouragement so deep, no challenge so formidable that we cannot overcome through prayer.

However, even in all Christ's intercession, the Spirit of God searches for intercessors. God wants us to participate in Christ's continual intercession. As Paul encouraged Timothy, "Therefore I exhort first of all that you make supplications, prayers, intercessions, and thanksgivings for everyone" (1 Tim. 2:1).

The greatest calling is to intercede for others. In intercessory prayer we call down the blessing of God and call forth God's purposes in the lives of others, to bless others as Christ did. He prayed. He prayed at all times and on every occasion. The Holy Spirit is given to us to lead us into this lifestyle of prayer, to help us in our weaknesses, and even to give us the words to pray. In prayer we will find the intimacy our souls yearn for in our relationship with Christ.

THIS INVITATION TO PRAY AND INTERCEDE IS OPEN TO ALL.

NOTES

INTRODUCTION

1. Larry Dugger, *40 Days to Defeat Your Past* (Lake Mary, FL: Charisma House, 2016), 1–2.

DAY 3—PRAYER IS A PRIORITY

1. From Mark 1:35–39.

2. "Capernaum," Biblical Archaeology, accessed December 7, 2016, http://www.bibarch.com/archaeologicalsites/Capernaum .htm.

DAY 4—THE SECRET PLACE

1. From Mark 1:35–39.

DAY 5—CHOOSING BETWEEN GOOD AND BEST

1. From Luke 5:12–16.

2. Dennis Jernigan, *Giant Killers* (Colorado Springs, CO: Waterbrook Press, 2005).

DAY 6—ALL-NIGHT PRAYER

1. From Luke 6:12–19.

DAY 7—THE KEY TO WISE DECISIONS

1. From Luke 6:12–19.

DAY 8—THE BEGINNING AND END OF PRAYER

1. From Matthew 6:5–15; see also Luke 11:1–12.

2. Blue Letter Bible, s.v. *"proskyneō,"* accessed December 12, 2016, https://www.blueletterbible.org/lang/lexicon/lexicon.cfm ?Strongs=G4352&t=KJV.

DAY 9—PRAY THIS WAY

1. From Matthew 6:5–15; see also Luke 11:1–12.

Day 10—What You Really Need

1. From Mark 6:30–44; see also Matthew 14:13–21; Luke 9:10–17; and John 6:1–15.

Day 11—He Is Always Enough

1. From Mark 6:30–44; see also Matthew 14:13–21; Luke 9:10–17; John 6:1–15.

Day 12—Never Alone

1. From Matthew 14:22–33; see also Mark 6:45–52.

Day 13—Be Still

1. From Mark 8:1–10; see also Matthew 15:32–39.

2. "Definition of Neuroplasticity," MedicineNet, accessed December 12, 2016, http://www.medicinenet.com/script/main/art.asp?articlekey=40362.

3. *Merriam-Webster*, s.v. "fervent," accessed December 13, 2016, https://www.merriam-webster.com/dictionary/fervent.

4. Ibid.

Day 14—Lesson Learned

1. From Mark 8:1–10; see also Matthew 15:32–39.

2. *Merriam-Webster*, s.v. "affliction," accessed December 13, 2016, https://www.merriam-webster.com/dictionary/affliction.

Day 16—Prayer Changes Everything

1. From Luke 9:28–36.

Day 17—The Miraculous in the Mundane

1. From Luke 9:28–36.

Day 18—Hidden Things

1. From Matthew 11:20–30; see also Luke 10:1–24.

Day 19—Humility Brings Endless Possibilities

1. From Matthew 11:20–30; see also Luke 10:1–24.

Day 20—Praying Like a Child

1. From Matthew 19:1–15; see also Mark 10:1–16; Luke 18:15–17.

Day 21—Faith Like a Child

1. From Matthew 19:1–15; see also Mark 10:1–16; Luke 18:15–17.

Day 22—Praying With Boldness

1. From John 11:1–44.

2. Yogi Berra, as quoted in "The 50 Greatest Yogi Berra quotes," Nate Scott, *USA Today*, September 23, 2015, accessed December 19, 2016, http://ftw.usatoday.com/2015/09/the-50 -greatest-yogi-berra-quotes.

Day 23—Expect Pancakes

1. From John 11:1–44.

Day 24—Suffering Has a Purpose

1. From John 12:20–50.

Day 25—Moving From Submission to Sacrifice

1. From John 12:20–50.

Day 26—Give Thanks

1. From Luke 22:14–23; see also Matthew 26:17–30; Mark 14:12–25.

Day 27—Gratefulness in Everything?

1. From Luke 22:14–23; see also Matthew 26:17–30; Mark 14:12–25.

Day 28—The Intercessor

1. From Luke 22:31–34.

2. "History of the Salvation Army," The Salvation Army, accessed February 9, 2016, http://www.salvationarmyusa.org /usn/history-of-the-salvation-army.

3. Ed Reese, "James Hudson Taylor," Wholesome Words, accessed February 9, 2016, http://www.wholesomewords.org /missions/biotaylor2.html.

4. "Dietrich Bonhoeffer," Encyclopedia.com, accessed February 9, 2016, http://www.encyclopedia.com/doc/1G2-3404700767.html.

5. "Mother Teresa," Bio, accessed February 9, 2016, http:// www.biography.com/people/mother-teresa-9504160#related -video-gallery.

DAY 29—THE POWER OF INTERCESSION

1. From Luke 22:31–34.

DAY 30—JESUS'S MISSION STATEMENT

1. Emperor Julian, as quoted in "Inspired by the Incredible Early Church," John Piper, April 6, 1994, accessed February 10, 2017, http://www.desiringgod.org/articles/inspired-by-the -incredible-early-church.

2. "What Were Early Christians Like?," Christianity.com, February 10, 2017, http://www.christianity.com/church/church -history/timeline/1-300/what-were-early-christians-like-11629560 .html.

DAY 32—IN THE WORLD

1. From John 17:1–26.

DAY 34—WATCH AND PRAY

1. From Matthew 26:36–56; see also Mark 14:32–52; Luke 22:39–53.

2. Blue Letter Bible, s.v. "pneuma," accessed February 10, 2017, https://www.blueletterbible.org/lang/lexicon/lexicon.cfm ?Strongs=G4151&t=KJV.

DAY 35—PERSEVERING PRAYER

1. From Matthew 26:36–46; see also Mark 14:32–42; Luke 22:39–46.

DAY 36—FORGIVING EVEN THE UNFORGIVABLE

1. From Luke 23:26–49.

DAY 37—FORSAKEN BUT PRAYING

1. From Mark 15:21–41; see also Matthew 27:32–56.

DAY 38—DESTINATION

1. From Luke 23:26–49.

2. Yuritzy Ramos, "College Students Tend to Change Majors When They Find the One They Really Love," Borderzine, March 15, 2013, accessed February 13, 2017, http://borderzine.com /2013/03/college-students-tend-to-change-majors-when-they-find -the-one-they-really-love/.

DAY 39—AN INVITATION TO INTIMACY

1. From Luke 24:13–49.

DAY 40—A FAMILIAR PLACE

1. From Luke 24:50–53.

CONNECT WITH US!

CHARISMA HOUSE

(Spiritual Growth)

[f] **Facebook.com/CharismaHouse**

[t] **@CharismaHouse**

[o] **Instagram.com/CharismaHouse**

SILOAM

(Health)

[p] **Pinterest.com/CharismaHouse**

MEV — MODERN ENGLISH VERSION

(Bible)

www.mevbible.com